Back to Brazzaville

Back to Brazzaville

Dan Whitman

NEW ACADEMIA PUBLISHING VELLUM

Washington DC

VELLUM An imprint of New Academia Publishing

NEW ACADEMIA
PUBLISHING

4401-A Connecticut Ave., NW #236 - Washington DC 20008
info@newacademia.com - www.newacademia.com

Author with motorbike, Brazzaville 1980. Congo River visible in the distant background.

Contents

Preface

They used to call them just "Congo-K" (Kinshasa, thirty million back then), and "Congo-B" (Brazzaville, two million). People could keep track. Then heads of state and diplomats made up fancy names for them and things got confused. After I was in Congo-Brazzaville in 1980-81 on a teaching grant, Americans back home told me I was "wrong," that I had lived in "Zaire" — the huge one across the River they knew a little about.

The Little Congo, contentious enough in its own troubled history, had its version of suffering. Nothing quite compared to the horrors across the river, where the British born "American," Henry Morton Stanley, inflicted punishment and death wherever he ventured. His own journals boast of executions honoring his arrivals in remote villages, and note his letdowns where none took place.

Damning Stanley as the Villain of the Congo often goes with contrasting judgments of the Italian-French explorer Pierre Savorgnan de Brazzà, whose less abusive style on the right bank of the river was more liberating. Brazzà himself was an emancipator, and purchased slaves to free them. Unfortunately for his legacy, the commercial interests following him left their own devastation. In *King Leopold's Ghost* (1998), American historian Adam Hochschild points out that by the end of the nineteenth century, the relative number of human deaths on both sides of the river were close enough to be a rounding error.

Central Africa has a history rich in empires, conquest, the traumas of European encroachments, community development. However, our sources on this largely depend on oral history and legend. The written version of events starts mainly with European colonization in the nineteenth century. Aside from a few Portuguese fragments, what preceded was mainly anecdotal.

It went something like this:

As far back as we can tell, three kingdoms formed a political order in the region: the Kongo, the Luando, and the Angola—the latter not to be confused with the modern-day state of Angola. The King of the Teke kept relative order until the arrival in the 1600s of the Portuguese, who by the 1680s had destabilized the region through devious alliances and commercial interference. Chaos and order competed.

Centuries later, explorers Stanley and Brazzà, competing but never quite in open conflict, staked out claims in the watershed of the Congo River. Both were motivated by the explorer's zeal to "discover" the unknown, similar to the drive of astronauts today. Getting there first also mattered.

By the time Africa was carved up at the Conference of Berlin in 1884, Belgium took the vast left bank of the river, and converted it into the personal property of King Leopold II. France took the right bank and positioned its trading center Brazzaville exactly opposite the Belgians' Leopoldville on the river's bulge still known today as the Stanley Pool. Today the only other sovereign states in the world within line of sight of each other are the Holy See in Rome, and the government of Italy.

During World War I, Africa became the staging ground for proxy battles on a continent that knew nothing of Europe's conflicts. A hilarious depiction of this comes in the 1976 French comic film *La Victoire en Chantant* ("Black and White in Color"). In its opening scenes, French and German colonizers in a fictitious country—Togo or Cameroon—coexist harmoniously, sharing picnics and holidays, until the day a ship arrives with backed up French newspapers reporting on the war breaking out in Europe in summer of 1914. The French community has an emergency meeting, and rises to sing the Marseilleise. *"C'est la guerre!"* says the self-proclaimed community leader.

"War? Who with?" asks a voice in the back of the room.

"Who with! Well, the *Boches* (The Krauts) of course!"

"Oh. I figured it would be with the English as usual," says the chastised voice in the back of the room.

The Germans and French in the contiguous colonies had no animus at all against each other. They engage befuddled locals to fight on their behalf, so as to demonstrate their patriotism while also staying out of harm's way. Their African underlings appreciate the idiocy of such a conflict, and perform perfunctorily under threats and orders. No one much gets hurt, and the bayonets forced on the reluctant fighters are never really put to use.

Books and movies set in Africa tend either toward the African or the European point of view. In this chestnut, the two blend and interact comically. On the sanity-vanity-inanity spectrum, Africans come out way ahead.

Histories of modern Africa generally begin at about this period.

But *Back to Brazzaville* is also a story about me. It goes with thirteen years on the road in the United States, showing African travelers the four corners of my country, and learning both about it and them. They were visitors chosen by U.S. embassies in their countries, sent as potential future leaders who would best understand the United States and its system, so as to interact more positively as mid-level ministry officials or professors or journalists. A few became heads of state. Of course we wanted them to like us, but short of that, at least to understand us.

One of my visitors told me how as a child, he had witnessed the French punishment for tax deadbeats in the former colony. With villagers present to teach a lesson, they would catch the offender's head in a wooden vice and tighten the vice until the head cracked. Aside from seeming a grotesque punishment for tax evasion by the penniless, this struck me as an astounding account brought from a period not all that long ago, from the lips of an observer to my ears in the 1970s.

At the end of our thirty-day study tours, some of the visitors would say things like, "If you find you're ever in Ouagadougou, look me up."

I arranged for this to happen in 1973, and made my way to the capital of Burkina Faso ("Upper Volta" of the time), and placed a phone call. My former travel companion sent his houseboy to the airport to guide me into the city. We embarked before dawn, and with the help of a bicycle the houseboy balanced my little suitcase on the handlebars as we walked together from the airport to the downtown. He set me up on the veranda, still before sunrise, on a chaise-longue where I dozed while waiting for the household to wake up.

I saw long-necked birds perched on the eaves of the ranch-style gutters, and said to the houseboy, "Ça c'est des vautours (vultures)?" I asked.

"Non, Monsieur," he reassured. *"C'est des pigeons."*

On other visits to the Continent I'd committed indiscretions, like the day I pulled out a camera to photograph a beautiful slope of nature. I found out the hard way that I was within espionage distance of one of the head of state's many residences. Uniformed guards jumped out from behind the bushes, machine guns aimed at my head and neck.

"Je vous arrête!" one said.

Local friends stepped in and negotiated to have me released. Money, untouched by the soldiers, went discreetly into their pockets. Later my friends explained to me, "We all knew how it would end up, we just didn't know the exact price until we talked it through." To me, machine guns aimed at me seemed nasty. To my local friends, they were just a negotiating position.

My reaction could either have been dread and a wish never to be in such a situation again, or the sort of intrigue that convinces thirty-year-olds of their immortality and eggs them on to further brushes with uncertainty. It seems I chose the latter, so when a chance came up for a lengthier stay in Africa, I put in my stakes and hoped for the best.

I applied for a Fulbright fellowship, this time for Brazzaville, and off I went in 1980.

Reader's Manual

This book includes memoir, history, recollections, drawn from experience, primary and secondary sources, and oral interviews. The two sections in "Civil War" citing comments from Ambassadors James D. Phillips and Aubrey Hooks are drawn from oral histories on line at the Academy for Diplomacy Studies and Training, with their gracious permission to reprint here.

I offer this mixture of genres with the hope that a less known land may show its depth, breadth, and antecedents. In its frustrations and unrealized potential, the country is dear to me.

Themes emerge: conflicts generally are power plays in origin, not the "ethnic" or "tribal" warfare we read about too often in cursory newspaper accounts of Africa's troubles; conflicts are managed, not "resolved"; loyalty is often opportunistic, with the agents of loyalty bearing odd mixtures of good, evil, and survival. If we seek "good" and "evil" as recognizable qualities, we likely fail to reach understanding.

I ask the reader's indulgence in tracking strands of the story. While the forms and times shift, the tale at least goes mainly in chronological order.

Dan Whitman
Washington, August 2019

Introduction

July 19, 2018. Thirty-eight years since I'd been to Brazzaville. Still three degrees south of the equator, but now unrecognizable. This time there was air conditioning, isolation from the outside, but also the loss of the smells and rhythms from before.

Gone, the sweetish smell of burning garbage, and the mangy thoroughbred dogs left behind by French aid workers and professors when they departed on their summer vacations in France. Gone also, the dirt thoroughfares, and the banging of metal on metal: third world sounds of people fixing things. Now even poor people just replaced their old, broken cooking pots with new, cheap ones, courtesy of the Chinese.

Not exactly Schliemann's Troy, it didn't have much underneath, the old buildings now dust from decades of civil war and urban renewal. Before the changes, it had seemed more a village than a city.

I was drafting schedules and funding requests in my embassy office. At first I didn't notice the stranger in my embassy office. I looked up when he said something. He didn't seem like embassy staff, but security wouldn't have let him in otherwise. He was about my age, maybe a little younger. Dressed in a simple, expansive local shirt and worn pants, frayed shoes, his African hair half grey.

"When I saw you in the hallway last week," he said, "I had the impression I'd seen you before. Is it possible you lived here in about 1980?"

Taken aback, I dropped my pen and offered him a seat. I got up from behind the desk and took the chair next to him. "Were you at Marien Ngouabi University at that time?" he said. "You look familiar, though naturally a little changed."

"I was there, yes," I said, a little suspicious. "Are you saying you were one of my students back then?"

"No, but I think I remember you from the campus."

"I haven't found anything here I recognize from before," I said as I tried to read his expression. "Do you know the little neighborhood where the profs used to live?"

"I do. Opposite the Marché Filbert Bourou, off the Avenue Simon Kimbangou."

I processed the moment. "Can you take me there if I get a car? Maybe Saturday?"

"*Avec plaisir,*" Michel said. He was a grounds manager at the embassy.

Here begins and resumes the story.

Back in 1980 I had lived in modest digs in an academic ghetto with an Iranian, Brits, French, an Italian, Soviets, and a Laotian as my neighbors. All taught at the university named after martyr Marien Ngouabi—the president killed in 1977. He had served as a national figure in a country slighted by history in being *given* its independence, rather than "winning" it. Neighbors who'd been there longer than I had disdainfully called the university "*le lycée,*" since its standards were not, shall we say, up to the Grandes Écoles in France.

My Congolese boss at the English department said, "We try to pass half our students." Repelled at the time by this harsh standard, I realized later that "half" was a generous, not draconian measure. The students were listless. In retrospect I think they may have suffered from malnutrition.

After a year and a half of trying my best, I took away lively memories. They come to me now as *tableaux vivants*:

> Sunsets over the gorgeous river, beer in hand, as the sky darkened at dusk. A hundred thousand vampire bats filled the sky, lifting off from their day jobs on the Île du Diable in the middle of the river, to the mainland where they would find cattle to feed on at night.

> Flan and coffee under the arcades of a colonial French marketplace. A child approaches and says, "*J'ai faim.*" I offer a spoon and a seat at my table; frightened, he runs away.

Community security guard Gabriel cooks *maboke* — vegetables and savory fish slowly roasted in palm leaves over an open-pit fire.

Afternoon run; amazed children laugh and point, "*Moundêlê! Moundêlê* (weird foreigner)!!"

Marxist street poster:
A hard life today for a better life tomorrow.

Graffiti covers the slogan:
A hard life in Bacongo [the workers' neighborhood] *for a better life in Poto-Poto* [the cabinet ministers' quarters].

Shower out of a blue bucket. Two gallons, plenty.

Civil servants will bring about the development of the country." [Graffiti added: "*Sure. Meanwhile, how about paying them?*"]

A train cuts through the forests of Maya-Maya to Loubomo, as if to the Auvergne.

Geckos stage acrobatics on the wall. Better than Cirque du Soleil.

A tarantula, big as a freight car, scuttles under my refrigerator to the cool shadows below.

A tropical rain cleanses the city, dust removed everywhere the next morning.

La clarification idéologique, c'est reprécision du dirigeant du parti d'avant-garde et la fidélité du Marxisme-Léninisme.

Pas d'unité pour l'unité!

Now in 2018 I was working a temporary job at the new U.S. embassy. The only building I recognized from before was Blanche Gomez Maternity Clinic, built by the Chinese in the late 1970s, when

China's per capita GDP was one-third that of the Congo. For lack of running water, the clinic was never used in the 1980s, and now still stood empty.

A new *corniche* led from Brazzaville's center to the Case de Gaulle, where the leader of the Free French held the Brazzaville conference of 1944, now the French ambassador's residence. Built by the government of France, the *corniche* connected to a bridge to nowhere—aesthetically eye-popping, donated by a newly prosperous China.

The dour Congolese from before seemed gone. Gracious, quick to laughter and easy to deal with, the "new Congolese" seemed to be on social media, able to access some personal funds. Even a Brooks Brothers outlet opened with fanfare during the second week of July. It seemed counterintuitive that this could have a clientele in a poor country of four million (up 100% from the 1980s) but Congolese assured me it would. "When they have any money at all, they spend it on clothes," an embassy driver told me.

Michel, the stranger in my office, took me out to the city that Saturday. We saw the Brazzaville crafts market, where you can come and go with no hassles, no pressure to buy, and an open and relaxed atmosphere. Again, unimaginable in the 1980s.

"Make an offer on anything in the store," one stand owner said.

"What I value most here is *you*," I said.

"You can't afford me. I eat too much," the stand owner said.

This sounded funny in many ways.

It seemed the new Brazzaville had pulled up its socks and was ready to join a wider world, held back only by air fare, visas, and enough reading material to meet its wishes. Michel and I scoured the city, discovering much that was new and nothing much from before.

In thirty-eight years, the country had gone through travails and traumas. Corrupting oil deposits abetted factional and regional disputes. North-versus-south edginess came to a head in 1992, with northerner Denis Sassou-Nguesso displaced in elections by southerner, anti-Marxist Pascal Lissouba. Lissouba quarreled with runner-up Bernard Kolélas. Fights broke out. The spoils went back and forth between the two as Kolélas got to be mayor of Brazzaville, then Prime Minister. Sassou meanwhile waited in the wings…. But we get to this later.

Now I see that the new "Little" Congo (Republic of Congo) hovers like a sting ray over a murky past. The civil war of 1997-99, politically inspired and, with ethnic overtones, took a steep toll in ROC. These days a teachers' strike shuttered the university, as professors went without pay for five months. As the market price of oil dropped, so did single-product Congolese exports, and with it, the local economy. Asked why they weren't paying their teachers, the government said it had "other priorities."

July 22, twenty juveniles, ages twelve to twenty-two, were rounded up in a police sweep targeting violent urban gangs; sixteen were detained. Something went wrong in the holding cell in Chacona precinct. Thirteen died overnight, maybe victims of a tear gas canister tossed in their crowded cell when they made a ruckus. The good news was, under public and media pressure the government owned up to the calamity three days later, and agreed to investigate. Even the government-owned Dépêches de Brazzaville carried the story as it developed, without spin. The cold war truly over, a VOA transmitter went up for local broadcast July 20, undoing decades of suspicion between ROC and the United States.

As with other African states, Congo-Brazzaville has a road ahead before realizing its potential. Connected, savvy, determined, its youth and an emerging entrepreneurial class may carry it forward, and certainly out of the doldrums from four decades earlier. Or failing that, get out and live somewhere else. It's best for all if they manage to make it at home, and maybe they will.

August 2018

[Introduction reprinted courtesy the *Foreign Service Journal*, October, 2019]

One

As It Was

French Equatorial Africa—AEF—had existed for less than half a century, 1910-1958, but in that relatively short time, French became lingua franca, ancient French engineering held the infrastructure together more or less, and Gallic rules of the road ("priority to the right…") were strictly upheld. Huge semi-trucks came to screeching halts at the traffic circles to defer to tiny Mobylettes entering to their right. The event of the week was the Tuesday night arrival of the UTA flight from Paris, loaded with third-rate camembert cheese rounds and stale croissants. All were sold out by mid-morning the following day. Obnoxious expats gave orders with the familiar "*tu*" to strangers in the streets, as if they hadn't gotten the memo about independence. On the other hand, French saints and sages embedded from earlier years continued their good works as church activists, teachers, and railroad officials as crusty and inseparable from the landscape as native born Congo-B sons and daughters.

The African capital of the Free French during World War II, Brazzaville was the venue for de Gaulle's planning meeting in January of 1944. Thirty-five years later, even as other African countries were renaming things and finding ways to remove painful colonial memories, the De Gaulle Croix de Lorraine kept its place of honor on a hill overlooking the powerful Congo River. Pierre Savorgnan de Brazzà, exploring for the French, had put up a flag in 1883 on the right bank of the river, proclaiming, "*Qui me touche sera libre.*" The unlucky ones, born under the Belgians, were promised freedom if they could make their way to the "French" side and touch the flag.

Arriving, Now Thirty-eight Years After

I alight now, 2018, to my new temporary home, a row house near the new United States Embassy — walking distance, in fact. Night noises. Toads, frogs. The toads are steadfast, as if desperate. I wonder if they may be courting me, for who else could be within hearing range?

I can't sleep for all the croaking. Nights later, after a long and loud neighborhood party scared them away for good, I realize I've gotten used to the sounds. Now I actually can sleep better with them than without.

In the mornings, the universal sounds of village roosters crowing, the clanking of tools on metal. Just as it was, thirty-eight years before.

Bacongo, 1980

The neighborhood called Bacongo had aspects of a Goldoni play, with comedy, conflicts of manners, and the passage of time. Our expatriate community sailed like a ship in mid-ocean: French, Chinese, British, Swedes, East Germans, Soviets, Americans and Italians jammed the gunwales, far from the conflicts raging on the mainland. We all shared problems of heat, noise, loose bowels, and thieves, and had to deal with the same, imperfect conditions. Rumors flew — the coup being prepared by the Soviets, the grandiose French development contracts, the unflattering UN Development Programme studies being kept under wraps by the government. But the stories didn't govern our lives, they only served as substitutes for the lacking contrast of changing seasons.

When I arrived in October to work at the university, the Soviets next door were poking at a car wreck on their front lawn, in a chassis that was its own coffin, up on blocks and lacking all four wheels, littered with spirally leaves from the tree above. The owners grinned at me optimistically, assuring me that the car would be working within a week or two, and helpfully point out to me the danger of using my motorbike in the aggressive traffic of the capital.

The rains came and went. The car, which anyone else could see had found its final resting place, was half covered with mud and rust. The Soviets spent the rest of the year on motorbikes themselves. They grinned at me again toward the end of the year: "Why the thieves aren't taking our car which we leave out for them? Why they only take our Mobylettes?"

Spotty, the cantankerous mongrel lodging with the British couple across the way, developed an unexplained interest in the Soviets' yard. He found ingenious ways of escaping from his fenced in area to go explore across the street. For a month, there was the almost daily spectacle of both Harrisons chasing their elusive Spotty through the yard of the socially aloof Easterners, and an aftermath of apologies from both sides. Once when the Soviets saw Spotty coming, they rushed out of the house and threw up their surrendering hands to the rest of us in the neighborhood with pleas of innocence: "It is not we who call him!"

The Western bloc neighbors made jokes about the microphone the Soviets had probably planted up Spotty's anus; the Soviets no doubt said the same about us. Perhaps World War III may yet be averted—or precipitated—by a Spotty who can't grasp the nuances of geopolitics.

The crisis uniting the neighborhood was our water problem. All of Brazzaville had failures and shutdowns from time to time, but our area seemed singled out: we had nothing at all for five months, and lived by expensive bottled water plus the few drops that came out of the neighborhood spigot in back of the Iranian Armand Natat's house. After trying to fix the situation a few times, the Water Works people just gave up on us. Occasionally we went to the chief engineer to complain, plead, and threaten, but we always lost heart as he pulled out his hydrologist's map of the district and promised to fix a certain feeder valve by the following Tuesday, and never did. We also knew he was lying, and that he had no idea what he was talking about, but there was nobody higher up to complain to. When an official explains why something is hard, that's a sure sign nothing will be done. What to do? A mile away from our dry kitchens and bathrooms was the second mightiest river in the world, after the Amazon. The Congo's average discharge is 1,459,964 cubic feet per second.

We came in, four or five of us, trying to intimidate, even when our forty cc mopeds didn't make much of an impression or even need mufflers. Roller Thunder we were not.

On days when the chief engineer had to show some serious intent to fix the feeder valve, two oldish laborers might appear at the main road in front of our compound. They planted the branch of a bush in the ground to show there were "Men Working." Sharing a single shovel, they dug around for an hour, as someone might do at the beach. They lost interest at about the time of the morning coffee break and just went home.

Four blocks down the main road, the powder-puff fountain in front of the French Culture Center insolently gushed water—rightfully *our* water. One Tuesday, just as we were about to carry out our threats and create public scandal by bathing in the French fountain, our own water lines were mysteriously restored. The reappearance of our water was almost a letdown. I had a nagging feeling that during all those months some feeder valve had just been left in the wrong position, like a switch in a railroad stockyard, and the Water Works people were just too embarrassed to say so.

July 4, 2018

As I did thirty-eight years ago, I hold Bach, this time also Dvorak involuntarily in my head through the Paris-to-Brazzaville flight. Call it boredom, anxiety, it puts me back to where I began.

On the plane across the aisle is a proud Congolese father, his child asleep in his arms. The map screen on the Air France flight shows Stanley Pool as we fly over it—a thrombosis on the River like a magnificent lake, but in fact it has a current that can drive you to your death on the shoals of its rapids if you linger in the center. Water lilies flow past like race cars.

Over the vast green of the land below, as the plane descends to landing altitude. When we say "France," we think of the French; when "England," the English; but when we say "Congo," people think of the River. Here is the paradox, with some tragic elements built in: they think of the place and its grandeur, not the humans who inhabit it.

Arriving at Maya-Maya airport, the procedures are a thousand times easier than at Dulles or Paris-De Gaulle. The border policeman seems to say "Welcome back" in his smile. "It's been thirty-eight years," I say.

"Well, things have changed."

At twenty-eight degrees Celsius, the evening air is breezier than Paris, much cooler than Washington.

Bacongo of 1980 was also a favorite lair for fraud artists collecting for bogus charities. They knew that no matter what our country of origin, we had more money than the Congolese, and probably more gullible "social consciousness" as well. Otherwise we wouldn't have been there in the first place.

One local imposter claimed to be collecting for the disabled. I gave him money the first two times, the third time I asked him to come with me as I checked his papers with the police. I hoped I wasn't standing in the way of getting bread to the lame, but saw my instincts had been right as the supposed Marcel Kassunvo dashed off through a hedge.

Some of us in the neighborhood—French, Russian, Italian and I—went to the police station to explain the incident and turn in the false papers the faux Kassunvo had been left with me. We were angry because we knew it would be awhile before any of us would give to any charity again, so the imposter had really stolen not from us, but from those who really needed it. The police chief ordered one of his officers to go pick up Marcel Kassunvo.

"If the man is an imposter, he's not about to put his real name on this document!" I said.

"Right," said the police chief. "The next time this happens, here is what I would like you to do. Leave Kassunvo in your living room—make up any excuse—and slip out and come to get a policeman to arrest him…"

"It wasn't Kassunvo, it was an imposter," I said. "You're suggesting… I leave a thief alone in house?" I said.

He scratched his head again. "*Ah, bon*. Good point. There may be a better way."

My international neighbors and I went out in our small Mobylette brigade to various places by the river. We went swimming, risking schistosomiasis, in calm waters near the rapids where the meandering Djoué empties into the Congo. The place was called the "*Plage des Russes*," in honor of a Russian who had drowned there.

Sunday evenings we rode far beyond the rapids to Tantine Jacquie, an outdoor bar where the Congolese brought their mistresses at dusk. From the slope we could see bats over a large expanse of the river. At twilight, tens of thousands of vampire bats took off from an island in the river, and flew high overhead on their nightly migration to the Congolese countryside to feed on the blood of any surviving livestock in the failing light. Their vast numbers, the grace of their wide arc in the sky, and the expanse of the land and river below all seemed contrived, like a sophisticated Hollywood creation.

After Easter that year, four weeks of political seminars at the university disrupted the courses we all taught there. The seminars came during the last six weeks of the year, when we could have used the time to make up missed work. Classes were cancelled, badly needed lecture halls were commandeered by the priority meetings. Even the Marxist tutorials were suspended the day they feted the anniversary of the renaming of the university after the fallen national hero, Marien Ngouabi.

People in our expatriate neighborhood, almost all connected to the university, began to crack one by one. Not that all were so enamored of the work, exactly, but we just wanted our existence to add up to something, after all the hot and rainy months spent making lessons plans and collecting bucketfuls of water at the outside spigot back of Natat's house. Now we lost patience with each other, with our community spirit, even our international banners.

The plague of seminars disrupting our teaching, and our friendly relationships, had been staged by local Party people for the benefit of the1000 Soviets in town; this was reasonable enough, as everyone knew the Sovs had picked the present regime and would also pick the next. I was curious to know whether the Russian neighbors, the ones with the automobile carcass, found any pleasure in the grey pageantry at the university those weeks. Following tacit rules of comportment in the neighborhood, I never asked.

Ange and Gabriel

Back in 1980 Gabriel belonged, serf-like, to two buildings in Bacongo, my own and the one next door. Incoming tenants respected tradition and hired Gabriel as their night watchman; he also had extra work with them to clean and do laundry. On special occasions he would make *maboke,* a Congolese dish of vegetables and fish wrapped in palm leaves and stewed over an open-pit fire in the back yard.

As a southerner, Gabriel had the usual bitterness toward the northerners who ran the country and were known for graft, incompetence and waste. Not since the Abbé Youlou, deposed in 1963, had the country been unified and free of sectional rivalry, said Gabriel. He told plausible stories about the few southerners who got functionary jobs in the north, who either got themselves killed, or else managed to return on foot, by night, never to go upcountry again.

Ange, the Frenchman next door, had Gabriel for most of the time. Ange taught geology at the university. He loved the Congo, which I guess replaced for him the parents he'd lost in France at an early age. He had students often to his house, and sometimes took them on week-long outings to the bush. He knew he couldn't abide a geology program with students who had never picked at rocks. Soil might as well be taught at the faculty of letters in that case, Ange would say, as if geology were some sort of poetry.

Night watchmen in Brazzaville slept through their shifts. No one faulted them for it; their presence alone was a deterrent. The idea was that the thieves, who were rarely violent, would stay away for fear of waking the watchmen. Gabriel performed like the others; only the difference was that he kept his family with him during his watch—Delphine and the three children. Ange seemed to like having them planted at his doorstep, as a substitute for the family he never had. The iconoclast side of him broke the tacit French rule of distance from one's servants. He fathered them, talked to them, had them eat from his table and bathe from his outside faucet when the water lines suddenly worked. Michel, the elder, was made to do homework at Ange's desk in the evening. Gabriel, the father, didn't like that.

Tension built up between Ange the Frenchman, and the venerable Armand Natat upstairs, over Gabriel's service, practice, and affections. Natat, a Persian with French passport, was the eldest and highest-ranking of several hundred French professors in Brazzaville. He had an ailing back and, in France, ailing children, and many worries. Natat, not Ange, had hired Gabriel when he'd moved in eight years earlier. It was he whom Gabriel loved in fact, called him "Papa," and named his second son after him.

Gabriel's family hung around abjectly at the landing of the building like refugees. Ange wanted it that way, but Natat didn't like having to step over them every time he came home and went upstairs. He couldn't understand why they didn't just stay in Talangaï, where he had built a house for them.

Finally, Ange and Natat differed and argued. Ange called Natat a racist, interested in the Congolese only as a curiosity. Natat, seeing the conversation and friendship ended, turned and walked away. From then on, you could then spend evenings with Ange or Natat, but not with both together.

One afternoon Ange had a half dozen of us to his house for a *maboke* Gabriel had cooked in the charcoal pit in the back yard. Gabriel had worked many hours over it. He wanted to please us, and did a lot of fussing over the charcoal pit. "I am an artist," he said. "When I clear a path, or do laundry or make *maboke*, it may look like I am only doing things. But really I am thinking."

It was one of Gabriel's better efforts, but Ange made him come and face us all as he criticized him for making it too salty. Gabriel was dismayed but thanked Ange for his candor. "Only through criticism can a person improve," he said. He stayed as the guests began discussing the weather changes in the area. On this, Gabriel was an authority. "It is not as in past years..." he began, but Ange dismissed him before he could finish his sentence.

"Gabriel always has an idea about everything," Ange told us, laughing loud enough for Gabriel to hear from the kitchen.

There were other problems between Ange and Gabriel. Ange the Frenchman had the children come in from the outside landing to watch television. Gabriel didn't object to television in principle, but was anxious about the French films showing white women whose bosoms, though covered, he found suggestive and corrupting. He did not like his children seeing them. He tried to forbid his little son Maurice from watching television, but Ange overruled him.

The tension grew. At Natat's insistence, Gabriel sent his family to stay more often at the house in Talangaï, but everyone knew they would begin drifting back, and they did.

Ange seemed at least to have a real fondness for the children. He took them to soccer matches and to plays at the municipal theater. He advised them, trained them, sent them on errands, paid attention to them. But he also trampled Gabriel's authority as a father. When Gabriel would step in to take the children away from the television, Ange always intervened. "Your father is a fool," he said to Maurice one afternoon after Gabriel had gone off, defeated, to return empty bottles to the market for reimbursement.

One night we were all woken up in the neighborhood by gunshots coming from the path back of us, near the science faculty. "*Y'a des voleurs dans le coin!*" said a voice from the house behind mine.

"There are thieves in the area!"

Then I heard Ange next door calling for Gabriel. I went out with a flashlight and found Ange, who asked me angrily if I'd seen Gabriel. "No," I said. "I guess he's chased away whoever it was."

There were different stories about where Gabriel was that night. Some said he was there all the time, in the shrubbery a few houses down, with the teenage girl he had with him for most of his night watches. He himself claimed later that he'd been hiding in Ange's garden, hoping to spring on the thieves and catch them by surprise. Delphine, aware of her husband's paramours and wanting to clean up his public image, swore he'd been home with her in Talangaï.

The remarkable thing about the row the next day was that it was Gabriel who went after Ange, rather than the reverse. He simply cracked under the strain of accusation, harassment, and humiliation.

It was hot that week, and tempers flared all over. Though the Harrisons hadn't had a fight for a while, the neighbors were conditioned to watch out for arguments that might end up in tragedy. In this spirit, I was summoned one afternoon by the Italian Delvalle to help separate Ange and Gabriel, who were arguing loudly and about to exchange blows. "I was married in a church!" Gabriel kept repeating in the thick of it, somewhat crazed. "Do you think I could tell a lie?"

The family—Delphine, Michel, Emma, and the little Maurice—drifted around listless on the landing of Ange's building. I had them to my house where we all drank soda and waited for Gabriel to calm down enough to join us. The four sat quietly at my dining table. They had seen these things happen before.

Then, from the silence, the twelve-year-old Michel expressed the first opinion I'd ever heard from him: "It is Gabriel who is crazy because Monsieur Ange is too kind to him."

"And what will happen with all this?" I asked.

"I hope Papa will leave, because otherwise he will do a meanness to Ange."

Weeks went by, tension grew between Ange and Gabriel; also between Ange and his upstairs neighbor Natat. Finally, Ange fired Gabriel just as Gabriel quit. Now Gabriel worked only for Natat, though he stayed on the payroll for the two in the building next door to myself and the Laotian, Arounothay. Now that Natat had more share of the authority, he insisted the family stay in Talangaï more often. Had he not built a house for them there?

Little Michel began disobeying more flagrantly, and came to Ange's house for camaraderie and television. Gabriel stopped giving money to his wife and children, now that they were estranged and living in another place. He began sleeping with the teenage girl more often than before, then he gave it up and slept alone under the shrubbery in the back, near the lemon grass. He sat watch by himself in the evening, reading comic books, gazing into the distance. Nothing penetrated his brooding and loss of self-esteem.

But Ange could not be said to have won the battle. On May 10, 1981, Socialist François Mitterrand was elected president of France. Brazzaville neighborhoods of old guard French expatriates decked out black crepe. Ange anguished and gnashed his teeth, and announced the lid being nailed on the coffin of Western civilization. He fell gravely ill and crawled to bed for the rest of the week, exhausted by life and, I think, his bungled dealings with Gabriel, Natat and the others.

Harrison

The Harrisons were the unhappiest household in the capital. Robert was with the British Council. His wife Isabelle was Gabonese, a former student from Robert's teaching days in Libreville. Our French neighbors had a way of getting upset over their brawls, and sometimes ventured out to find a way for international diplomacy or local police to intercede. But there was no British embassy to help the Harrisons, and the UN Development Programme and American embassy had cut themselves loose and would have nothing to do with the pair, even though they did speak English. I didn't feel as extreme about them as the others did, and was usually willing to help them and be helped by them, in the way neighbors were with one another.

Robert and I were the two English teachers at the university, where teachers seldom taught, students never studied, administrators didn't administer. All the expatriates had their ups and downs, but Robert had moments of deeper spleen than the rest of us, maybe only because he'd been there longer.

The Harrisons' arguments were difficult for us English speakers, because we could see that they were excellent neighbors when sober. The day I sprained my ankle running, they sent over Isabelle's live-in niece Rebecca with an ankle bandage. Whenever they went on a weekend drive up one of the two passable roads in the country, they would come to fetch me first, taking the south road to Kinkala and an African restaurant there, or, less often, the north road to the beautiful pine forest past the town cemetery.

One day on the north road we laughed each time the same bicyclist passed us while we stopped at one drinking place after the next. I think the bicyclist even made it back it back to the city before we did at the end of the day. On our outings we would eat, joke, and argue. The arguing Rebecca and I left to the two others. I would gaze at the passing scenery, waiting for the dispute to taper off; Rebecca with her somehow unscathed psyche would draw on her eleven-year-old savvy and pretend not to understand, since the more violent arguments usually took place in English.

I liked Robert for his intellectual liveliness and his willingness to explain to me, the newcomer, the ways of the university. He read incessantly and drank liberally—two practices Isabelle found unpardonable. Although Isabelle had no children of her own, she had most of the virtues of the African mother: the patience, the verve, the prevailing good cheer, the unquestioning generosity. But she leaned hard on Robert, interrupted otherwise tranquil evening conversations with sharp rejoinders: "You're drunk, Robert," she would say, accurately enough, making him sidestep her remark in order to keep the conversation both sociable and intellectually plausible

According to legend, their first brawl had been sixteen years earlier on their wedding night in Libreville. Since then they had generally fought about once a week. The violence mounted, hovered, exploded cyclically, like the tropical storms around us. Every evening with them was a study in antagonism. They kept no secrets, and displayed before me and others both their present domestic skirmishes and their recollections of past ones. No reaction, pity, or interventions were called for; the innocence of the observer and neighbor was always respected. We others served as involuntary tribunal, usually swaying in favor of Isabelle for whatever it was worth, because of Robert's tyranny over her (she was not allowed to work or travel). But we were granted neutral status. The Harrisons were no fools, and knew that without these rules of neutrality for guests, no one would ever visit them.

The morning after a night of crisis, Rebecca was sent across the unpaved patch to fetch me. I found Isabelle in her room, just emerging from a sort of paralysis which the previous night had affected her whole body, but which now immobilized only her fingers. I listened to her account of the row, saw how she tried to move her hand without success, and promised to look into "medication" for her paralysis. I left her room and passed the demarcation zone into the territory Robert took as his own during their crises, namely, the back patio facing the Bacongo market. Robert sat serenely with a beer and a book. He and I chatted for a while, then I brought up Isabelle's paralysis.

"What she needs is a placebo," he said. He was right, of course. I went home, got unmarked vitamin pills for Isabelle, and gave her fake, precise, and slightly complicated instructions on how and when to take them. My quack's cure took effect within the hour.

Robert and Isabelle were both large; Robert had a terrifying goatee, copied off a Hogarth painting. Looking at him, I could imagine him warming his feet in the bowels of a serf after the hunt on a cold day in Northumbria. For most of the day he was compassionate, trying to do a conscientious job. Only, it was true, he was a demon when drunk, which he reliably was every day after sundown at six o'clock. Then the moral and demonic halves vied for mastery over him; it was poignant to see him at time when you knew he was doing his best to get control of himself. He had a false front tooth whose cap wandered around in his mouth; the sign of the demon coming out was, along with the reddened face, the black hole in his mouth, and the cap eluding the searching tongue as the tongue chased it around the palate and cheeks.

I think one of the Harrisons' problems was the closeness of their house to the Bacongo market. Directly across the road was the record stand. The salesman there seemed to have only one record: the same tune came over the loudspeaker all day at a cruel decibel. There were also transport buses and militia vehicles passing by on the main road, honking at close range. I brought back ear plugs for the Harrisons from my trips back to the States, but I think they never used them.

In describing a recent battle, Isabelle would point to scars and bruises on her face and arms, the work of former brawls with her husband. Twice she'd been hospitalized with an eye bruised shut and then again with dental surgery to repair damage to her jaw and the loss of two lower teeth. But the pair was well matched: she was no less husky than Robert and was likely the cause of *his* wandering front tooth.

They liked to shut each other out of the house. In our neighborhood houses had metal grills that were locked at night to keep thieves out. One Harrison in the house at dusk might close the grills on the other; the other would wake up the neighborhood with screams, then settle down for the night in the car out front. On one of these occasions Robert managed to force his way into the house; Isabelle was waiting for him there with a can of gasoline and a match; she doused him and lit the match; the fire spread up his shirt sleeve before eleven-year-old Rebecca managed to smother the flames with a bath towel. In his drunken state, he noticed neither the fire nor the extinguishing of it.

I missed one memorable lockout. They fought in the car and Robert pushed Isabelle out onto the street far from home. She spent the rest of the evening in cafés. Later when she came home, she took a wooden plank to the car, breaking all its windows and mangling both fenders and the headlights before Robert could get out of the locked gate to stop her. They didn't even bother going through the usual, preliminary phases of exchanging insults and threats. Rebecca had seen the signs of the more serious brawls coming on, and that night collected up all the knives and blades in the house and deposited them at the French neighbor's until things calmed down. Unfortunately, she forgot to hide the gardener's machete. Isabelle found it in time to use against Robert as he defended what remained of the car. She cut a nice gash his forehead, and was preparing to finish him off when the neighbors overpowered her.

When I returned home that evening, Isabelle came over to describe the skirmish. She had gotten Robert, it was true, and the shattered car was the talk of the town for the week; but he'd managed to land a couple of good ones on her as well, and now Isabelle's face was pudgy with purple and scarlet areas. She told me she'd made secret plans to leave the country with Rebecca.

"It's about time," I said. "I don't see how you put up with this for sixteen years."

"I would have left long ago," she said. "But, how could I? Robert wouldn't allow me to work, so anywhere I went had to be paid for by him. Also, when I married him I gave up my Gabonese citizenship, so I had nowhere to escape to. Just to make sure, he went to the Gabon embassy to make them never give me a visa."

"Can he do such a thing?"

"This is Africa. It's how things are done."

"Then it doesn't look like you're going anywhere."

"This time I am. I have a friend Robert doesn't know about at the embassy. He's bought a ticket I've been hiding for several months, and also arranged to get me the visa."

"I'll miss you, but it's time you left."

"All I'll do is wait for Anne Marie's visit next week and then in ten days I fly the coop."

As I listened to Isabelle make excuses about why Anne Marie should visit, I knew Isabelle would never leave. She had permanent need of Robert.

I was one of the few in Brazzaville who tolerated the Harrisons. Other than myself there was only a Congolese police officer who visited occasionally, and an Irishman who had been in the city for eleven years. Why did I continue with them? Their openness, and their liberal permission to me never to have to choose sides. There was also the pleasure of seeing Rebecca, proof of a child's resilience in adversity. She nicknamed me "Diplodocus" during a time when she'd been reading about dinosaurs in school. I drove her around Brazzaville on the back of my motorbike, discovering her child's sense of humor. "Were to next, Timbuktu?" "No, Peru!" "Kalamazoo?" "Dienbienhpu" "Shall we see when the next train leaves for Geneva?" "Too bad, nothing there until next Tuesday."

The neighbors hated the machete and gasoline incidents. But I looked forward to seeing the family as I returned from my spring break out of the country. When I stepped off the endless flight from Paris the following week, Robert and Rebecca were waiting for me, had consulted the air schedules and appeared at my door to greet me just as I came in from the airport, to invite me over. By the time I went across the way to see them, Rebecca had gone to bed, Isabelle was out somewhere, and Robert had started drinking. "The trouble with you and your people…" he said belligerently. I took my tired self, and my now ebbing tolerance, across the way back home.

The lockouts continued over the next few weeks; one night the neighborhood was awakened at three by Robert trying to get into the house. Isabelle had locked herself in and managed to destroy the key. "But who is going to open this door?" Robert kept shouting in English, in his high-pitched drunk voice. Then we heard thumpings and shattering of glass, and a French neighbor calling out into the night, *"Eh, ooh. Silence!"* as though to whining cats in heat in the alley.

Rebecca's schoolwork meanwhile had gone from mediocre to bad during the year, and she was not invited to stay at the school the following year.

"The headmistress is not unsympathetic," explained Robert. "But she said Rebecca, who is already in a class of pupils older than her, cannot remain without affecting the others adversely."

Robert walked in my door uninvited one evening as I was sitting at my dining room table with Albert, a Congolese colleague. Interrupting us aggressively, and drunk, Robert demanded to know what we were doing, as if it mattered: what were those papers we were looking at? What sort of outline were we writing? I was about to leave for dinner with other friends. I said I could explain later when I had time. Robert refused to leave until he got "a full explanation." Albert and I got out and left Robert behind in my house. When I returned after dinner, Robert was gone but the papers were scattered on the floor.

The next morning Robert apologized abjectly for his "inexcusable behavior last night." He isolated himself for several weeks, his better half wanting to spare the neighbors his demonic side. His behavior was touching—saintly, almost. The few times during those weeks when anyone saw him, he refused to drink anything but cold water. He acted with a new sense of reserve, never again really threatening or bothering anyone in the neighborhood. Rebecca, out of school, returned to Gabon; Isabelle came and went quietly, going to market, visiting on the other side of town. The record salesman at Bacongo market found a new tune and played it at a lower volume. The French neighbors began to nod good morning at the Harrisons' house as they passed in the unpaved street.

But finally I'd had enough. I started locking the gate outside of my door even when I was at home. I never had any of the Harrisons to my house again, and never went to theirs.

Langues Vivantes Etrangères

The department of Foreign Living Languages was my academic home for the year. It was heavy on the English courses, which all students wanted to learn. Less so, for the others.

Two years earlier in 1978, Sylvain Bemba, a Congolese writer and luminary, had been the first official visitor to the United States after the period following 1973 when the war in the Middle East had resulted in diplomatic break-offs by a number of African states. "Normalcy" came back five years later. Bemba and I had traveled through the United States and become friends.

Bemba was the éminence grise of Brazzaville's university—a writer and philosopher of an earlier generation—and my point of contact when I arrived two years later in October of 1980. He always received me with open arms in his dingy office at Bayardelle-Marien Ngouabi. In 1980 he was preoccupied, sleep deprived, anxious, afflicted with worry and marked by the limits of what he could do in that noble but striving, underfunded institution. When U.S. Ambassador William Swing had given some modest funds to the Congo Ministry of Culture, no strings attached, Bemba said to me, "What the Soviets give us are pads of paper by comparison. The day Ambassador Swing leaves us, we will all be orphans, *mon vieux*, orphans!"

Soon after my arrival in Brazzaville, public affairs officer Bob Murphy guided me to my university-provided apartment, a modest little unit on the first floor of a two-floor building, with a large yard front and back, filled with sprigs of grass, about six varieties of trees including a *flamboyant,* and generous amounts of lemon grass in the back. Something like the Garden of Eden, the lemon grass—*citronelle*—was always plentiful for a quick clip and some boiled water to make a fragrant tea.

We went to meet Jean-Pierre Ngole, the chair of the English department and my new boss. In his cramped and cluttered office, colleagues came and went, shaking my hand and welcoming me. Ngole and I worked out my teaching assignment, which ended up being grammar, comprehension, a bit of American literature, and a composition class. Twenty or thirty were to send written assignments in by mail, in what was then a correspondence course.

In my academic neighborhood I went next door to introduce myself to the Soviets. "*Pure* American?" they asked playfully. "What percentage American?" They talked about the relative worth of physicists and chemists at the university.

I defended the physicists: "But it is you who come to launch the rockets, no?" The Soviet answered, "Without the chemists, we'd have no fuel for those rockets, and then, where would we be?"

I saw our next-door relations would be tolerable at least, friendly at best. We never got much beyond that.

The Saturday of the week I arrived in October, President Sassou left on a state visit to Angola. The same afternoon, small airplanes dropped leaflets over the city. With a rudimentary photo of the president, the leaflets offered the type of slogans I later saw plastered on poster boards throughout the city:

1980 Année de test pour tous. (1980 Test Year for all).
Pas de pardon pour les saboteurs, les détourneurs; pas de pitié pour les essoufflés, les paresseux. (No forgiveness for saboteurs, embezzlers, no pity for those who are worn out or lazy).

On 28 October, two neighbors and I went out on our Mobylettes to explore. On the way I captured more slogans from the billboards dotting the city in place of the commercial ads which were prohibited:

Produisons d'avantage pour asseoir notre économie (More production to secure our economy)

Nous travaileurs, serons sans pitié pour les saboteurs de notre économie (We workers will show no pity for the saboteurs of our economy)

Le centralisme démocratique c'est l'autorité indiscutable de la direction du parti qui a caractère électif. (Democratic centralism is the indisputable authority of the party platform of an elective nature).

I found these slogans exotic, a little far-fetched, and more Chinese than Soviet in inspiration. I wrote them down when I came across them in public places. In retrospect they can be seen as quaint period pieces, parodies out of the films of Jean-Luc Godard of the same period.

As I went on my visits to the university, I saw that dear Bemba was generally troubled and went nights without sleep, I think from the insomnia of anxiety. Bemba had been close friends with the late minister of information, who had accompanied the head of state in 1962 to meet with President Kennedy. Later Bemba's friend dragged his feet on some of the more fanciful propaganda messages he was ordered to deliver to the world. He was accused of treason, tried, then executed by firing squad. This left Bemba rattled, staying in his house for a year, reading. By the time I met him, he'd been put in charge of cataloguing periodicals in the university library. Everyone knew he was, in addition, one of Congo's notable writers and thinkers. When I arrived in 1980, he was always friendly but reserved with me. He knew any false step would have consequences with the regime.

My colleagues, all good-hearted, had identical résumés—all had been to the United States on Fulbrights, all had done dissertations on African American protest literature of the 1960s, and all had put their theses in the context of a failed American capitalist system. This they imparted to their Congolese students as required by the local government thinking. The minders were not persistent or sophisticated, but they could make spot checks at any time and undo a person's career or life span. My colleagues supported and welcomed me, even when the administration of the university went a bit lame, taking three months to get the school year even started, and confusing teaching schedules and assignments. The snafus were not political so much as administrative.

My language courses seemed pretty acceptable at the beginning, including large numbers of beginners—some motivated, some not. I found that dictations helped the students judge their own progress and diagnose their needs. I sensed that my manner in involving them in the pedagogical process was something new to them. They reacted positively.

Meanwhile on November 24, I tried to find out when the Christmas break would be. I went to the rectorate to try to get some idea of this, and was sent to four different offices to find out more. I entered an empty room and soon enough found an official, the personnel director, screaming at me for my impudence. "You must first go to the secretary!" he said, though I'd already done so multiple times.

I said, "Monsieur, you must have slept poorly last night."

All the expats knew that when conditions became rough, they always had the option of folding their bags and going home. This made us more intrepid.

November 27, Thanksgiving Day that year, there was a coup in Ouagadougou. All followers were taken aback, and reminded that countries and regimes in the newly independent countries were on a slender string.

That same day, a Belgian in the UN Development Programme told me that there was a "fierce battle" going on between President Sassou and some of his own army officers who believed he was not energetic enough in furthering a Marxist-Leninist program for the country. Whether he was or not, Sassou survived the period and went on to lead for many years, a pragmatist who said and did whatever he needed to stay in control.

December 4 the body of a sentry was found floating in the River behind the American Embassy. The body was too bloated to fit in an ambulance, so they had to break the legs to get it to fit. That day many of us learned that sentry duty is not a sinecure. One night when there seemed to be prowlers near the residence of an American diplomat, the sentry on duty locked himself in an outhouse to hide from those he'd been hired to fight off. Later he fell asleep there. Security was no simple matter.

I kept visiting Bemba, concerned about his mental state. He seemed more drawn and exhausted, and in time his worries mounted as his mother entered a terminal state. Even in the most trying times, he made it a point of honor to be the first to arrive each morning to tend to his files, at 6:20 a.m. when all were supposed to be at their work places, though few were.

My journal entry for Friday December 12: "A chilling revelation: in this country where the general health seems relatively good, the number of people with atrophied legs is conspicuous. As someone pointed out the other day, it is almost always the *right* leg. This, perhaps because of a series of shots hitting the sciatic nerve twenty years earlier, by well-meaning nuns. Gruesomely plausible."

The Meetings

In the Department of Living Languages we had occasional faculty meetings, sometimes to discuss obscure aspects of French grammar (In a compound sentence, does the adjective agree with the noun in the dependent or independent clause?) but occasionally drifting into more practical questions of meeting spaces and work assignments.

My Soviet colleague, teaching Russian language, glanced at me the first time, smiling reservedly. It could only have been irksome to be a Soviet in a developing country, the year the USSR invaded Afghanistan on shady pretenses.

One day the subject was the "crisis" in the masters program, where students were openly critical of the way in which it was run. Their teachers, in turn, were disdainful of the students' complaining. I listened but was otherwise uninvolved. One faculty member, envious of the one who was the chairman, contradicted him forcefully many times, and argued that *"travaux de recherche individuelle"* should rather be *"...individuels"* to agree with *"travaux"* rather than *"recherche."* This seemed a little arcane for discussion until it came clear that he intended to unseat and replace the chairman.

That year, not a single masters student completed the course. Jealousies came to the surface and I was glad not to have a stake in any of this. We found out that masters students received 20,000 CFA francs per month stipendium (about fifty U.S. dollars) which was something, but nothing much compared to École Normale students who received about twice that amount, or the Institute of Science, Education, Sports, and Development (INSSED) students in the harder sciences, who got ten times more. The humanities track was trouble, and filled with infighting.

By early January I was exasperated with my students of English, and gave them an unannounced quiz to demonstrate to them that they weren't doing the work. The happy outcome was that the quiz showed many *were* prepared for the exam. We then discussed aspects of a story I had assigned for reading. I saw that they hadn't exactly understood the overtones of the text—not because they hadn't read and studied it, but because cultural obstacles came in the way. A person leading an empty life in an American city was meant to seem sad, uninspired, lacking in spark. The students saw the character rather as "selfish." This was a discovery for me, in a place where mere existence was seen as a gift.

January 12 very few students came to class. Later I learned why: private municipal buses had increased their prices by twenty centimes (about four cents U.S.), with a cascading effect that taxi drivers did the same. This was later known as "the Fula-Fula affair."

Bus and taxi drivers were denounced as "anarchists" and outlawed. Backed into the secondary consequences of the Fula-Fula affair, and coming to terms with a number of my students not likely to pass the course, I understood my redefined mission in the country: help the few who might benefit and leave the others be. The major changes needed to make an acceptable living standard were beyond the scope and means of individual workers, and certainly beyond mine.

I spent evenings in my quarters, watching geckos stalk their moths, playfully, gracefully. The praying mantises advanced across the concrete floor with Latin, swaying rhythms, rhumba-like. I pondered how young Congolese had been denied the legitimate needs they had, even to be students. I knew I could help but not solve the problems

Meanwhile…

Un amiral sans troupes n'est rien
(An admiral without troops is nothing)
En avant pour le redressement économique
(Forward for economic recovery).

And the crowning one:

Le cadre doit dépasser l'esprit de clan et de la tribu, dût-il être rejetté par cell-ci pour se retrouver dans la patrie, la nation encore en formation certes mais de manière irréversible.
(Generally untranslatable but something like this, "The official must transcend clan or tribe, even though it may result in being consequently rejected by the latter, so as to find himself in the mother country, a nation still in gestation certainly, but irreversibly.")

Week of the Moped

February 6 the French neighbor Ange was mangled in a moped accident, came back to the neighborhood with his face swollen, his hand not working, and with a limp. He was mostly interested in telling the rest of us the *kindness* of those who witnessed the accident. A Congolese motorist had stopped, made sure Pétra made it to the clinic, then packed the mangled moped in his car to transport it to a shop for repairs.

We all gathered at Ange's front steps to discuss the incident, and to wonder aloud about local politics. Some thought that Jacques Joachim Yhombi Opango, former head of state 1977-79, might get a ministerial portfolio under the Sassou regime. I didn't know enough to have an opinion on whether this would be good or not.

What I kept to myself was the other neighborhood event of

the week: the theft of my moped from the front of my house when I'd left it there (locked but unattached to any post) for a couple of hours. I knew as soon as it happened that there would be no point in grousing about it.

Even the day after my moped theft, I learned of another one for sale in the next neighborhood, for 95,000 CFA francs, about $200 U.S. I went to the house of the person selling it. I was glad to have it, though it had only half the power of the missing one.

I went to the police station to get the new one registered, and the police warmly greeted me from seeing me the day before. They seemed determined to achieve the impossible, and locate my missing one. Everyone knew this was a fantasy, and that stolen mechanical goods were usually broken down for parts and never seen again.

Not a week later, the police managed to find my moped, I don't know the circumstances or the way they did so. Surely it was mine, the same Mobylette, same color, the same scratches on the side. It was like finding an old friend. Whether they pulled fingernails or bribed witnesses, I'll never know. It couldn't have been webcams since there was no such thing at that time; nor electroshock, since the police station didn't have electricity even on a good day. The fatal flaw of the thief had been to drive the moped down to an empty gas tank, where it just stayed in the street since there was no way to take it further to break it down for parts.

I didn't press charges, and the police were rightfully proud of their achievement. For a week, I was the most famous expat in Brazzaville. Surely the country was on its way to development.

Bayardelle

They had names like Bahonda Philomene Aimée, Ndzila Grégoire, Tchiouanbou Marie-Jeanne, Ondongo Gaston. African names generally put the family ("last") name first, with the first-name handle afterward. I kept a register indicating "shows promise," "times showed up out of seven," "spot test," and *partiel.* Thirty in one section, fifty-six in another, forty-one in the third. Add to that the correspondence students, lab sections, and third year sections, and the total came to about 200. It wasn't easy to get to know each of them based on only weekly meetings, but I tried. I graded them on class participation, quizzes, exams, and general interest. Being a whimpy northeastern liberal, I sought to rank each student highly, but I ended up giving "shows promise" notes to only about a third of those registered.

Bayardelle was the section of Brazzaville where the Université Marien Ngouabi campus was. There were no toilets on campus, I don't remember how students and staff relieved themselves, but I guess it must have been in the dusty urban corridors of the surrounding streets and dirt paths.

The students generally showed reluctance or skepticism, which I later understood. No one explained to me at the outset that students were assigned to career paths by the Marxist central authorities. Those with ambition wanted to study law or business, but some were relegated to humanities and languages. Not many of the latter were there by choice. The ones designated by central authorities for the humanities felt themselves the underdogs. In fact, the only "over" dogs were those somehow related to the regime by blood or connivance.

The truth of it was that students were victims, like anyone else, of a broken system which worked for the benefit of an inner circle willing to pay obeisance to Marxist ideals and personal connections.

I was charmed by the undergraduates, but puzzled at their low output—now due, I realize, to political accommodations they had to make, and also a dulled intellect which could have come from the inescapable heat, or even lack of protein in the zero-to-two year growth period of their infancy.

A group in the back of the room performed dramatically better from the others—I learned later that these better ones were Chadian refugees. I didn't know the variables at the time, but it was unmistakable.

I looked forward to my weekly meetings with these large groups, and always wished the meetings were daily rather than weekly—a language cannot be learned in an amphitheater with sixty-some students only on a weekly basis. But the room was available only rarely, and was often overtaken by the sessions of ideological training for future Marxists. About a third of the time, I was told at the last possible minute that "my" amphitheater was taken over by the political rallies. Time lost to English instruction, I lamented. But these were the conditions of employment.

One afternoon in the campus courtyard, advanced students

came up to me and asked what they should do, now that their professor of American literature was MIA. He hadn't show up for two
weeks. I wasn't sure how to advise them, but then learned that their
prof had skipped the country without telling anyone, after getting
a Fulbright grant to spend a year in the United States. Not an hon-
orable way to go.

I reported to the language department with this information,
then got permission, myself, to teach the advanced literature course
which now had no instructor. I didn't realize that underpaid professors covered for one another, and looked aside as their own
colleagues did double dipping to make ends meet. I see how this
was a reasonable survival mechanism, but just didn't know how
it worked. So, when I volunteered to teach a course that was on
the books without a professor, I had no idea I was undermining a
system of compensating underpaid teachers so they could get minimum wage. I naively sent for a MacMillan anthology of American
literature and plowed through it with advanced students. These
dozens were far ahead of the 200 I had for basic language instruction, and made the job fun.

When we encountered harsh readings in our book—Puritan
sermons calling for the annihilation of Native Americans in the
seventeenth century—I apologized to these young intellectuals affected by colonialism. These accounts—the first instance of American "literature" in the form of sermons—seemed likely offensive
to intellectuals with recent memories of colonialism. The students
said, "No, we like this material. It shows that some people actually
believed in something. We never see this in our current political
leadership."

In retrospect I see my contribution to learning, if any, was that
I actually showed up to the classes I was assigned to teach. Not so,
the others in general. Coming onto the Bayardelle campus by moped, I often saw Congolese colleagues walking to work. I offered
them rides on the back seat of the moped.

Sometimes they accepted, though saying, "Let me off before we
get there. It's important no one see me, as profs are supposed to get
around in cars, not mopeds. The thing is, we don't have the salaries
to buy cars, so we walk." I wasn't paid much in my Fulbright teaching gig, but it was enough to make me a moped owner, a leg up on
my Congolese colleagues.

My basic language students learned what they learned, not

much and not quickly, but about half of them could demonstrate some progress during the course of the semester. Only later did I learn that they had no interest at all in learning any foreign language, but hoped somehow to survive on campus so they could keep their very meager scholarships and put off their encounter with the labor market which offered nearly nothing.

When the prof on the lam left a whole group abandoned and the department asked me to grade their exams, I gave it a try so as to be a good team player. The course had discussed Bernard Malamud's *The Assistant*, a dark story of dystopia in New York's poorer neighborhoods. The exams were noteworthy in articulating the party line, which was that Malamud was a perfect example of the failure of capitalism. It was obvious that Marxist catechism had established the intellectual platform for their reading.

I found an indirect contact to Malamud in New York at the time, and copied out by hand a few of the comments made about him.

He answered.

His letter to me said, "This is the year of *The Assistant* as examination material. It is being used by the French in this year's *aggrégation*, and now here's your letter with news from the Congo.

"I think the best statement I've read on my work—eloquent and unarguable—begins 'All and sundry righteously consider Frank Alpine as the main character in Bernard Malamud's book *The Assistant*.'

"Otherwise the statement is not bad because it moves in the direction of the truth.

"Thank you very much for informing me."

Maya-Maya

The airport road was the only one in the city with functioning street lamps. Students made the best of it, pacing back and forth with books in hand, maybe memorizing them, but also taking in the rare luxury of electric lights to read by at night. "Night" of course began at 6:00 p.m. with the sudden, tropical dusk and darkness. By 7:00, 8:00, the more studious ones were out on the Route de Maya-Maya in nearly perfect silence. It could be that they imagined better times and gathered their energies in those meditations.

There wasn't much to do in the evening in Brazzaville, so the expats went out to Maya-Maya airport once a week for a beer and a look at the departing planes. Big airlines didn't want to overnight in tropical Africa, so the schedules usually brought the big passenger planes in during day flights, then departed the same night.

Back then there was UTA, Air Afrique, and others. The expats had nicknames for them: Air Afrique was *Air Affreux*, Air France was *Air Chance*, Air Zaire was *Air Peut-être*; Sabena was *Such a Bad Experience, Never Again*. Even famous ones like TWA which never made it to Brazzaville became *The Worst Airline*. The only one that seemed to escape ridicule was Aeroflot, maybe because it had a bad safety record and it seemed unsporting to pick on it. The Soviets had a significant presence in the People's Republic, and enough back-and-forth with Moscow to have two flights a week.

The Christian aid official Lou Zopf was saying once that he'd recently been on a Russian plane. "An Ilyushin?" I said, trying to sound knowledgeable. "No," said Lou. "An actual airplane."

The neighbors would take the moped brigade out to Maya-Maya just before dusk, sometimes Ange came along, sometimes Robert, Natat the Iranian, Luigi the Italian. We would sit at the airport bar nursing a beer and waiting for an early evening departure, usually only one plane on a given day of the week. The roar of the engines and the drama of the takeoff became the day's entertainment. Not that we necessarily wanted to be on those departures ourselves, but they seemed eventful in a city where nothing much happened. The bartenders and barmaids got to know us and understood we were there for the distraction.

There might have been one movie theater in the city, and yes, there was a stage, but films and plays were rare. Local restaurants closed down early, and going to the one French place with six tables, le Mistral, was a treat for special occasions. There the chef would take the daily *capitaine* direct from the river and sear it a couple of hours later with a light sauce and steamed local string beans. Quiet, meditative. No piped in music to break the mood or conversations at the few tables that had customers.

Distractions were few, televisions very rare, and of course internet was not yet even a subject of science fiction. The short-wave radio did not entertain, but informed. A couple of times a day, from BBC or VOA or Deutsche Welle. Otherwise the book was what kept the mind engaged. To this day, reading in Africa was a pleasure now rare in a world in a hurry, with Wi-Fi connections going everywhere.

Back then you would read Thoreau at about the same speed as his own writing, say a chapter a day. The material became embedded, and reading was not sequential or "transactional." It was the way to anchor a mind in the tropics, cicadas rustling and sounding off in the lemon grass out back, and the occasional steady rain at night which went at a mezzoforte, neither diluvial nor sprinkling. The rains were decisive, gentle. Rain was considered good luck in the Congo, a sign of fecundity.

What would seem like tedium in big cities to the north was the baseline of the known daily rhythms. The pace welcomed anyone willing to adapt to it. Expats grumbled, complained, missed their home countries, but were not easily pried out of their drifting. Some stayed for decades.

The airplane departures at Maya-Maya reminded people of a wider world outside, and of little Congo-Brazzaville's status as a pawn in the proxy conflicts of the Cold War. No one actually in Brazzaville was much engaged in global rivalries or cultures in conflict. The Soviet neighbors were in it as much as anyone else. During my afternoon run on the day Ronald Reagan was elected in 1980, one day the Soviet next-door neighbor overtook me in his Lada on the dusty path to our academic village. He stopped with the window rolled down, and with an immense smile said for all in the neighborhood to hear, "*Je vous félicite pour Reagan!*" The reader may remember that at the outset, the world was astonished at how a mediocre Hollywood actor could be the elected leader of a large democracy. Having even lesser characters now in the twenty-first century shouldn't obscure the shock of the Reagan election.

Sweating and smelly from my run, I reached into his car with my own wide smile, taking on the Soviet's challenge and in my laughter granting him a small win in the global power rivalry none of us took too seriously. As if to say, "You got me this time!"

I joined in his laughter and went to my simple flat to "shower," using the water of a single bucket, filled over the communal tap over a four-to-five-hour period. Then back to the living area for the 7:00 BBC news wandering in and out of pitch in the blurry frequencies of the short wave. The little jingle identifying them in the 1970s was a small orchestral setting of an English folk song, intrepid and light-hearted. I found it comforting, frankly more so than VOA's "Yankee Doodle" handle. The radios, too, competed for the minds and hearts of millions all over the world with little electricity, much

isolation and unreliable water sources. They contributed to a platform of plurality of voices and ideologies and a Tower of Babel not
so murderous. The Helsinki Final Act of 1975 had left a stalemate if
not a state of calm over a bipolar world that now seems straightfor-
ward in retrospect.

No nostalgia for the Cold War! But at least the lines were drawn
and after the Cuban Missile Crisis of 1963, everyone knew that the
total conflict all were prepared for would likely never happen. There
were cruelties on both sides of the proxy wars, but the nastier Central American wars of the 1980s, or Balkan ones of the 1990s, were
ahead in the distant future. Genocides raged in Southeast Asia, but
there wasn't enough information at the time to make them vivid as
we now know they were.

During the three-month Falklands War of 1982, it seemed worth
it to navigate nightly to the hotel by the river that had a television.
The local Congolese newscast had no video sources or foreign cor-
respondents. Without the benefit of text or reader, the news an-
nouncer would indicate with his wooden pointer on a wall map
of the Southern Atlantic the approximate positions of the British
warships, and the locations of the deadly raids both inflicted and
suffered by the Argentine colonels so wastefully. He did this entirely from memory.

BBC in one of its finest moments intentionally downplayed the
drama, often leading in its evening news the commercial and financial developments or even local village politics in UK, before turning to say, "...And today, British naval vessels engaged Argentine
patrols with loss of life..." The cool temperature they maintained,
and almost total lack of rhetoric, gave them an exalted credibility
which I think no news source of today can claim.

Today Maya-Maya is glitzy and efficient, courtesy Chinese en-
gineers, and is in fact better organized than North American or European airports. Admittedly, there is less traffic to monitor. But no
one would go there these days just to have a beer at the departure
area and watch a plane depart. I don't mean to say this is a loss.
However, the camaraderie of the old Maya-Maya, while it may reappear yet in embellished forms, has vanished. And students now
have better alternatives than walking under the street lamps at
night struggling to understand or memorize their homework.

Kouyoumontzakis

In my study one evening in the Bacongo suburbs, I heard a scratching at my window. In the dark I couldn't see who it was. Then Bob, the embassy's public affairs officer, put a flashlight on his own face, and asked if I could come right away to a theater downtown to do some interpreting for a cultural event.

A Lakota Sioux dance group had arrived in Brazzaville, and were meeting with the Ballet National du Congo. Someone had thought there could be interaction between them, maybe some cross-fertilization of dance moves and a fusion of art forms.

Not all art is meant for blending. Even with best intentions and with plenty of talent on both sides, the techniques were not getting through. What seemed like some pretty basic moves on the part of the Lakota group were evading the Congolese, and vice versa. The idea was to have them choreographed separately, then together, at a public performance.

It just didn't work. The moves by each seemed simple, and I even tried doing them myself to help get the idea across. But I'm no dancer and the whole thing was falling apart. Someone had thought that one folklore could harmonize with another. Not so, though feelings didn't seem hurt and there was lots of laughter.

At the prep session I saw the problem: the African dancers did everything from the hip, the Native Americans from the ankle and foot. Neither could get the hang of the other. This was not a major problem during the performance, since the local audience was stupefied, fascinated, to see Native Americans in their exotic garb. The separate performances were dazzling, the combined one a comic fiasco. No one cared, and the whole thing was enlightening and fun. These Africans and these Native Americans had never seen one another close up. The audience loved the whole thing.

After it finished, a Frenchman in the audience came up to me. He was Georges Kouyoumontzakis, an engineer working on infrastructure projects on loan to the government of Congo-Brazzaville. He was eager to speak with the Lakota group, and needed me as French-English interpreter. He invited the six dancers to his house for a meal the next day. They went, and so did I. There I met Georges's wife, daughter and son.

Later Georges took me into his man-cave study, and showed me his fancy telescope for star gazing. Along the walls were relics that looked like pretty authentic renderings of Native American crafts, Lakota in particular. Georges had never been to the United States, but attended a gathering in France each year where French people exchanged information and artifacts relevant to the Lakota culture in particular. This seemed an unlikely coincidence, but in fact hundreds, maybe thousands of French people attended these gatherings.

Georges displayed for me the peace pipes, weapons, ornaments he'd crafted by hand, and showed me the French manual describing how these things were put together. An amateur endeavor, but not amateurish. It was in the making of them, he said, that they had authenticity. Certain kinds of feathers, leather, and wood were imported from the U.S., for use by these French craftsmen. I'd never seen a culture so intricately following in the footsteps of another, without prior contact of any kind.

This man was an eccentric to be sure; his enthusiasm was infectious. He stopped short of importuning anyone who might give in and have a look at his collection and workshop. The family saw him as something of an oddball, but as I got to know them over the months, they had the lightness and harmony of people of the South—in this case, Marseille. There was always a joke and some food, occasionally a swat to keep the son in line or I guess to make him "manly." Georges was macho, but the family took it in stride.

Months later I visited the Kouyoumontzakis family in Marseille during summer break. Georges took me down the main street of the city—maybe the rue de Lyon—and spoke in ominous terms of the thorough segregation of French from Arab neighborhoods.

"On this side, all French," he said. "On the other, we call it '*Petit Algers.*'"

He was troubled that this was happening in his Marseille, and very pessimistic about a future where the populations would be so separated. Assimilation was not happening, not even a little. North Africans had their reasons for leaving their countries to be in Marseille. But love of the French didn't seem to be one of them. Unfortunately, the feeling was mutual.

You could say he was a prophet of sorts, noting the cauldron of incongruities twenty-five years before the capillaries ruptured and riots broke out all over France in 2005, from Paris to the suburbs, and to many of the provincial cities. You could say Georges was a xenophobe and maybe years later he might even have voted for Marine Le Pen, I don't really know. But he was prescient.

The family loved their lives in Congo, and were among those who reached beneath the surface to understand the context they were living in. This was part of the paradox of colonization: the colonizing nations and their descendants benefited from a perverse political and economic relationship, but also turned more than a few of the Metropole individuals into keen observers and able anthropologists. At their worst, the French were cruel and predatory. At their best, more than a few took their foreign sojourns as opportunities to engage, share, observe, admire, and understand with humility the cultures they found themselves in. No pat answers.

Arounothay's Tux

Arounothay was a survivor of the Laotian holocaust of the 1970s. An economist, he was my upstairs neighbor at the university apartments. It's hard to imagine a more misplaced individual, but he was teaching economics in a Marxist country. Marxist in name only. Of the horrors of the twentieth century, the Pathet Lao in Vientiane were up near the top in cruelty and murderous social engineering.

There were two units in the little chalet we shared. I lived on the ground floor, Arounothay on the floor above. Modest but tidy. With the running water stuck in the city's antiquated pipe system. Like other expats, we respected one another's buckets. Half a bucket a day for washing dishes, showering, and boiling corn and rice. It wasn't all that bad. I usually got the morning shift at the neighborhood tap, Arounauthay got the afternoon one.

Arounothay was always cheerful, usually laughing about one thing or another. He walked around in a small bathing suit, which he called "my tux."

The story went like this: He had been director of the electricity company in Vientiane before the Pathet Lao took over in 1975. He'd been sent to one of the internment camps where few survived. His wife was taken to another. After a year or so of enslavement and daily beatings, he withered to a skeletal frame. Even when I knew him five years later, he was so small he seemed like half a person.

They had labored in the fields and then were taken to shout Marxist slogans in the late afternoon before getting their daily, single, tiny bowl of rice. "Louder, louder!" Many starved, others were killed with garden instruments and firearms. No one expected to make it out alive.

One day they found Arounothay in the fields, and managed to identify him. The Pathet Lao had realized they didn't know how to run an electrical plant, and retrieved him from the camp to get him back to his former work.

They spent a few months taking him around in a limousine and feeding him to fatten him up. It was no honor to be picked out of a death camp, and was also ominous since the regime was capricious. They told him to just sleep and eat and mind his business.

Even during those confused days he wore his bathing suit, which he called *"mon smoking."* His minders in the regime drove him through the city but never told him if his wife was alive or dead. It would have been pointless to ask.

After a few months getting him back in shape, they put him back to work at the electricity plant. No illusions here: perform or die. Arounothay used to laugh as he told me his story. It was the Third World laughter you can find anywhere, directed to irremediable hardship. It was also from his good nature.

One day his wife was delivered back to him without explanation. She'd been in a separate camp, and had also defied the odds and survived. They walked together one day near a bridge over the Mekong River.

A Canadian diplomat came up to them and said in a very soft voice, "Go now, cross the bridge, and we will pick you up on the other side. Just go now."

So it was that Arounothay and his wife made it out of their homeland hell, to Vietnam, and somehow from there to France.

In the 1960s Arounothay had done an advanced degree in economics, so the French government picked him to do a *"coopération,"* teaching in Africa so as to keep a hand in the former colonies.

He had learned conventional econ—macro, micro, market forces, things like that. This did not jive with the national university of a Marxist country. He taught what he knew. I thought for sure he would be expelled from the country. I kept a low profile myself, teaching English language.

"I'll be fine," he used to say, always laughing.

"But the bureaucrats here don't like what you're teaching," I said.

"And what if they don't."

I knew that Laotian death camps were worse than expulsion from the Congo, but still I thought he was being a little foolhardy, and told him so. He would always answer, *"Ne t'en fais pas,"* don't worry about it.

His stories evolved until he came back to the house saying that a few of the advanced students had told him they liked what he was teaching, and could he please tell them more.

Gradually his Western concepts took root until the junior Congolese faculty members showed an interest as well. Eventually, market economics came to prevail in the department. This was concerning to the political officers running the university. "Oh shit," I thought.

He was convoked to a sort of inquisition, and ordered to explain himself.

"I know Marxist economy," he told them. "If it's the Marxist catechism you want, I know I can do it better than you, since I did it on my knees for hours every afternoon in the camp in Laos. But if you want real economics, keep me here and I will provide it. Your choice."

Exasperated, the Authorities let him be, and he made it through a three-year stint as a French employee in the Université Marien Ngouabi. He built a following for himself.

Then he packed up and moved back to a suburb north of Paris. I visited him there a few years later. "You have done marvelously," I said.

"I still have my tux," he said. "The one I wore in the camp, and around the house in Brazzaville." It was cold in Paris that day, but Arounothay's smile was the same as it had been, four degrees below the Equator.

Sony

Sony Lab'ou Tansi, *né* Marcel Ntoni, came from a village near Kinshasa, Belgian Congo—now DRC. Born in 1947, he learned French only from the age of twelve, when his family of nine moved across the River to Brazzaville.

He raced through life as novelist, playwright, producer, civil servant, poet, and *enfant terrible*. Before his death of AIDS in 1995 he published two dozen novels, plays, essays, opinion books, winning the Concours Théâtral Interafricain de Radio-France Internationale (1979), the Grand Prix Littéraire d'Afrique Noire (1983), the Palme de la Francophonie (1985). The prestigious French publisher Seuil published six of his books, which had wide readership in France and Francophone Africa.

I had first met him in the United States in 1979, when he came on a study tour for African writers. I was the chauffeur, interpreter, therapist, BFF, mixologist, travel agent and cultural intermediary for four of them. In the good days of Operation Crossroads Africa, I was entrusted with a few elements of the travel arrangements for the thirty-day tour. I went out on a limb by taking my group of four to the northern New Hampshire hamlet of Sugar Hill. We spent five days in a small way station called Sunset Hill House, which might have been a stagecoach hostel in earlier days. The lodge had a sweeping view of northernmost New England slopes—ski slopes in the winter—with uninterrupted forest foliage spanning in every direction. Sugar Hill had crisp nights, intense late summer afternoons under a cool sunlight, and home-cooked meals decades before microwaves were even known up there.

It was fiddlehead season, a mountain fern which looks like tiny asparagus. Fiddleheads are harvested only in early autumn and steamed and served as a side dish. I remember René, the Togolese writer in my group, going into a sort of trance as he tasted his first fiddlehead, with the synesthesia of the intoxicating view of the mountain slopes opposite the picture window in the small dining room of the inn. I don't think I have seen any person as happy.

Sony was having verbal dustups with other members of the group of four, and one afternoon disappeared into his room to stay there for almost three days. I thought he was sulking. I didn't want to intrude, but wondered if he might have died. He didn't show up for our car trips through the area, nor for the meals at the inn. He was a moody artist after all. I hoped he might emerge after calming down or letting some sort of rage dissipate.

Emerge he did, after three days. With a broad smile he announced he'd sequestered himself in the room finishing the first novel of his which later got international attention—*La Vie et demie*. Paris: Seuil, 1979. When I picked up the book a year later, I saw it was signed at the end, "Sugar Hill, New Hampshire," and included a wink to me in a later chapter with something called the *rue Whitman*.

Later that trip we went to a poetry reading at Brown University in Rhode Island, where an elderly and retro francophone writer from the Caribbean dramatically read his own tiresome works to a captive audience in a vintage campus building. The poet's pretense was painful. As he gazed far into space to dramatize a line of his alexandrine verse, people in small numbers took the opportunity to slip out of the room and escape. I sat with my four African visitors, all trying to maintain some respect but glancing at our watches.

At one point the poet read his line, *"Ne fermez pas la porte!"* (Do not shut the door!), referring to an object of unrequited love, the generic kind almost required in neo- and pseudo-Romantic poetry.

Coincidentally at the same moment, an undergraduate grabbed his chance and slipped out the door behind the poet at his lectern, closing it on the way out. Sony sat next to me, his arms crossed, nodding vigorously to the line *"Ne fermez pas la porte!"* Instead of busting a gut laughing, he shook with suppressed laughter as if to say, "Right. And when do we get out of here?" and "For you I'll keep my composure, but not for much longer."

Sony was a great visitor. He absorbed, shared, went through phases of isolation and camaraderie. Friends of his had been executed in Brazzaville in 1977 on trumped-up charges of conspiracy, and he was furious. He knew well the people on both sides of the river had been betrayed by their leaders (Mobutu on the one side, Sassou on the other). Most of his works were harsh parodies of misrule in Central Africa, inspired partly by Alfred Jarry and the French Theater of the Absurd, but with large doses of originality and local rage. The local references hit a nerve in his expanding reading public, and had a decade or so of notoriety in the francophone world. *State of Shame, A Life and a Half, the Antipeople, The Eyes of the Volcano, Who Ate Madame d'Avoine Bergotha?* were some of the works later translated into English.

We stayed in touch. When I came to Brazzaville a year and a half later, he stopped in to see me often, made sure I was getting around the city, took me on short excursions, and attended the readings and events at the American Cultural Center attached to the U.S. Embassy. He was busy all the time, and had to check in once in a while after all, at his sinecure position at the Geographic Mapping Lab of the Ministry of Science and Technology.

A month after I arrived in Brazzaville in 1980, he picked me up one day in a borrowed car, and took me with two African friends out to the Pont du Djoué twenty kilometers beyond the edge of the city. A drunk soldier with an AK-47 stopped us and made us present papers. Sony winked at me in the back seat and said, "Watch carefully." He handed the military man his own photo ID through the driver's window, thanked the guard and took it back. Then he passed the same card a second, then a third time for the two other Africans in the car. The guard was too drunk or addled to notice he was getting the same ID for three different people. Then it came to me, clearly of a different complexion. With a wink Sony gave the same ID a fourth time to the guard, who then waved us on.

It was good fun to the three Africans in the car, scary to me since the machine gun could have been loaded. All in our thirties, we took this prank and risk as reinforcement of our illusions of immortality.

Sony produced Alfred Jarry's *Ubu Roi* brilliantly on the Brazzaville stage, to hip and knowing audiences. I told him that while he was at it, he might as well stage *Macbeth*. Everyone would get the message, and you can't exactly censor Shakespeare. Sony liked the idea but never got around to it.

At an international conference in Nice some years later, he was asked about the use of the French language among African novelists leaving aside their native languages for the more universal one. The question came up all the time in the 1970s and 80s, and I do remember one visitor on the opposite side of the polemic, saying, "Ewe [a language of coastal Benin and Ghana] is an international language. If delegations at the United Nations want to communicate with us, they will have to learn Ewe." Good luck with that.

Sony was disgusted with these arguments, and championed the use of a language, French, he only began to learn at the age of twelve. Communicate with the wider world, he said, or just stay in perpetual isolation. It was daring to say so at the time, only shortly after the independences when pan-Africanism came with thick ideological packages.

Answering the question that day in Nice with controlled rage, he said, "Believe me, we learned French. It was strictly forbidden to speak local languages in school. When they caught you doing it, the punishment was to wear a small box tied around our necks, with shit inside. Shit in a box. We learned, and learned well. And so should everyone else."

Brazzaville had its almost ancestral literary figures: Sylvain Bemba, Blaise Bilombo-Samba, Emmanuel Dongala, Henri Lopes, Léopold Pindy, Jean-Pierre Makouta-M'Boukou, Jean-Baptiste Tati

Loutard, Tchicaya U'Tam'si, and in fact at least seventy-nine authors published in the 1970s, a good share of them internationally. This, in a country of two million. Sony took his pen name "La'bou Tansi" as a tribute to his mentor Tchicaya U'Tam'si, who likewise wrote about grotesque injustices by the local regimes in the subregion.

A hot summer evening years later in 1992, my phone rang in Washington and Sony took me by surprise by being in town, invited me to a café near Dupont Circle to meet one Bernard Kolélas. They were looking for funding for an election that year, and trying to get Kolélas elected president. They represented something called the MCDDI, the Congolese Movement for Democracy and Integral Development. I asked if they were "progressives" or "socialists" or "liberals" in the European sense.

They looked at each other and shrugged, then Sony said to me, "We have no idea. We are just for the full flourishing of the human being."

My naïve heart went to them, as my money would have if I'd had any. Never mind that Sassou's PCT Works Party won all 153 seats in the People's National Assembly, with a very unlikely 93.64 percent (sic) voter turnout. According to government stats, not even Kolélas voted for himself, since the only dissenting votes were either "mistaken" or "blank." I never saw Sony or Kolélas again.

He won a seat in parliament the following year, and would have represented the Brazzaville neighborhood of Makélékélé. Newly elected president Pascal Lissouba (maybe the only one ever truly elected in Congo-Brazzaville) took a dislike to him and had his passport revoked. Unable to get medical treatment overseas, Sony tested positive for AIDS in 1994. When his wife died of the disease May 31, 1995, he followed fourteen days later. He never reached the age of forty-eight.

Today in Brazzaville the main cultural center in the city is the Centre Sony La'bou Tansi, which has a stencilled image of him on the outside wall and conducts readings and plays such as he would have wanted, marked by rage and lethal humor.

Voice of… Reason

There wasn't much to do in the capital in 1980.

The Soviets had just invaded Afghanistan, and my English language classrooms were taken over about half the time for political rallies to curry favor with the Soviets. The students didn't care much one way or the other. They were affable young people looking for a meal, a job, and a night's sleep.

The Pushkin Institute offered free Russian lessons, paid for by the Soviet embassy. I didn't much like what the Soviets were doing outside their borders (or inside, for that matter). But that wasn't the fault of their beautiful language.

The U.S. embassy had directives not to associate with any of the thousand Soviets in the city. I wasn't part of the embassy, but stopped in anyway, to get guidance. Bob, the American public affairs officer said, "Well you're a private citizen, so I see no issue with this. If you want to do it, just go ahead."

I showed up at the Pushkin Institute, a small property which a half dozen classrooms, where the lingua franca was French. I asked if I might take one of their introductory courses. They responded with simple generosity and openness. "Here are your books. The course starts Tuesday."

I said, "I'm a U.S. citizen, if that matters."

"Why would it matter?" the kindly registrar said. She handed me a stack of free books almost too heavy to carry away on my moped.

The weeks went on and I learned a few words and phrases in my class of six or seven. I didn't like the slow pace of my learning, but knew it was only from my own lack of discipline. I was beginning to get the hang of it, and could even follow a few stories. The teachers were astute, and the Institute was a tightly run shop.

The more of the language I learned, the more I saw it as a tall mountain, my own learning curve a small bump on the steep incline. Plus, the ambient French was an easy fallback when words failed me.

Those were the days when BBC, VOA, Deutsche Welle, Radio Moscow, Radio Netherlands, and others competed head-to-head for attention on short wave channels. Each had an "Africa Service" in English or French, and came on with comforting regularity at news time. VOA was a stitch with its "Special English" (like the joke that ends, "Well in that case, let me tell you... verrryy... sloooowly...").

BBC had the strongest short-wave presence locally, and its news programs were dry, professional, reliable, and always on time. Anyone who listened back then will remember with nostalgia the fading and strengthening short wave signal, the artful tuning it took to pick it up solidly, and the lovely English country tune it played to announce news time. And the beep-beep-beep to mark Greenwich Mean Time, now sadly renamed "Universal Time."

Radio Moscow had its biases, but I thought it might help my language learning if I spotted it on the short-wave channels. As the story goes, "If you want to learn a language, just go somewhere and find a proselyte. Probably you already know the spiel by heart, so you'll catch on as it comes to you with foreign words."

I would listen to BBC at home, sometimes VOA, to get a pretty accurate version of the world's tumults. Then I would try to tune in to Radio Moscow to hear their version of it. I could pick it up pretty easily in English, but never quite got the frequency for the original Russian. Curiosity set in, and I wanted to speed up my language learning.

We gathered in the courtyard of the Pushkin Institute after class one afternoon, with students, teachers, and even the director, chatting in French. Russians, Congolese, French, the rare Italian and myself, we were all there to tackle the language from one angle or another.

The Institute director gave me a friendly glance, so I said, "I've been trying to find Radio Moscow on the short wave. Would you know the frequency by any chance?" Mind you, this was during a tense period of the Cold War, as the blundering USSR stepped in way over its head in Afghanistan and was later stung badly doing so.

Without hesitation the Institute director said to the fifteen of us gathered in his courtyard, "How would I know? I listen only to the Voice of America."

All laughed and mounted their mopeds to get home before dark.

I think back to the reckless friendliness of the moment, taking a breather from global conflict and differences. Just people in a courtyard. This, I am sure, is how to win hearts and minds, whether you deserve it or not. Way better than repeating a message until it flattens from overuse.

An Ideology

Marxism never much worked anywhere very well, but you have to admit, it was an intriguing model. Maybe the murderous run it had in the twentieth century was an unintended demonstration of how venal people are when given a chance under any system.

Even at its worst and most cynical, it was at least born of intentions. The system in Congo-Brazzaville gives a bad name even to the crudest formulation of this idea.

Congo produced the world's best avocados, pineapples, mangos, papayas, greens, even grapefruits. Unfortunately for the Congolese, these items went beyond the purchasing power of most families, so they went, mainly to expats, who snatched them up in the open markets before the Congolese could.

Hunger was a daily condition for most people, and manioc "outsmarted hunger" (*tromper la faim*) by giving people a sense they had eaten when in fact they'd only taken the equivalent of wood pulp into their systems. If you could find and afford some curry or hot sauce to dash on top of your manioc meals, it gave added advantage to escaping hunger. But still it was only an illusion.

In 1980 a man in Brazzaville figured out how to breed and grow chickens, which give the double protein benefit of both eggs and meat to humans. Bad for the chickens, but useful to humans in bringing out their inner energies. The man built a chicken coop, modest compared to the industrial production scale in virtually every country in the world.

Chicken generations click by at a pretty brisk pace, so the entrepreneur was able to multiply the numbers and mass of products which the public eagerly bought up. For a brief moment Congolese got protein into their diet, and the difference showed. Chicken and particularly eggs were affordable even to people on very modest budgets, so their children grew and learned and developed in better health.

The business lasted about two years until the statist government found out what was happening. Governments "sense" greed and envy. In the case of the Congo, where they fail to produce anything much for their people, they wreak terrible vengeance on any private sector investor with the gall to show that people can do things better than systems can.

In the case of the chicken farmer, the sabotage came in the form of a law forbidding the importation of chicken feed to the country. Hence the death of that business, and the end of affordable protein for the people. The government did this not with the intention of doing better for itself, but simply of keeping anyone else from doing what it failed to do.

Beggar thy neighbor. If the genie offers a wish, ask for something bad. Then, double the misfortune for your neighbor by wishing him twice the curse of your own.

This, then, a parable for how the centrist government made ultra conservatives of its people. They were never permitted to express these opinions in the form of elections or political choice, but quietly remembered the entrepreneurial roots of their own culture. Nor would they imagine they were "conservatives," they knew only that their state was sapping their energies and ideals and aspirations. Unwittingly they were Reaganites, because they believed the state was more the problem than the solution.

No one (no one) took the Marxist catechism to heart, it was clear in the graffiti on the poster boards dotting a landscape where commercial messages were forbidden.

But the wags defaced them with their delicious sense of humor, risking imprisonment and other punishments. Fun is the last right to be removed by oppressive systems. The Brazzaville system was not murderous or genocidal, not even violent in general. But it lowered like a dull cloud somehow making even the brilliant Equatorial sunlight seem grayish.

On the occasion of the twenty-third Communist Party Congress, garbage trucks fanned out over the city with decals on their rear bumpers, "Follow me to the XXIII Party Congress." The Central Post Office erected an immense billboard over its façade saying "Down with Envelopes [the slang word for bribes]!"

Congolese could be robbed of their livelihoods, youth, aspirations, health, and dignity—but not their humor. In this, they equalled the wags in the Soviet Union of the time, who expressed lively humor despite the penalties for doing so.

"You are accused of calling Brezhnev an idiot."

"But Your Honor, we all know that is true."

"No issues with that. The problem is that you have revealed a state secret."

Whole volumes attest to the vitality of Russian jokes in the darkest of times. The Congolese had no affection for Russia or the

USSR, but they rivaled the Russians in their ability to laugh at their circumstances.

Students all wanted to study in France or the United States. Houphouët-Boigny, the pragmatist ruler of Côte d'Ivoire at the time, was once accused of sending more students to the Soviet Union than to France, where they all wanted to go. He answered, "When I send them to France, they return as Marxists. Those who go to the Soviet Union return as capitalists. That's why I send more to Moscow."

The United States had no particular interest in Congo-Brazzaville in 1980, nor did France have extra cash to dole out scholarships. So most of those studying abroad reluctantly went to Moscow. Virtually all I spoke with said that the first Russian word they learned was "*obez'yano*," the word for monkey.

In the Congolese maternal clinic I visited, young mothers were packed two to a single three-inch mattress. I couldn't exactly see them through the dense clouds of flies that blocked the view. I sensed people veiled behind those dense flying raves, never understanding what was so appealing to the tens of thousands of flies that filled the area. They blocked even the view of those in the rickety beds behind. I was stunned at the disgusting conditions in a clinic serving people so badly, worse than an open field would have been.

Marxism was a marriage of convenience with Moscow. The Congolese government got basic military equipment and Russian lessons, a green light to proceed with a common agenda. Some meager resources went into some pockets, the people got essentially nothing. The tale is known to those who study the Cold War. In USSR, people got education, free housing, meaningless jobs, cheap reading and a good medical system. For the Congolese there was none of this, just submission to those who got there first for Russian handouts.

Maybe the perpetrators actually believed in what they were doing (though personally benefiting just in case). The citizens wanted only a bit of protein, and the fantasy of a way out. My colleagues in the language division at the university had been among the few lucky ones at least to taste the advantages of life abroad, on the condition that they toe the Communist party line when they returned. Those who had been to the United States were all specialists in the literature of capitalist greed and failures. They did so because it was the way forward for them and their careers and their families. I might have done the same.

Jeffrey Sachs at Columbia meanwhile worked diligently to become an authority on development, advocating that assistance be doubled in order to have positive effect. Economy first, democracy later.

Bill Easterly, his rival and antagonist at New York University, said, Baloney: democracy first—otherwise all efforts at development will fail.

History has all but proved Easterly right and Sachs wrong. But I will leave that debate to others.

Natasha and Misha

It seemed proper for Misha and me to glower at each other from across the table, at the meetings of our little language department at the university. The Sovs had just invaded Afghanistan on shoddy pretexts, sending the Cold War into yet a gloomier moment. Brezhnev, often pickled, had to be propped up during public appearances. It was normal enough for Congolese to be learning Russian and English, but there we were in the room together and didn't know exactly what to make of it. I'd met Russians before, but not an actual *Soviet.*

Fraternization with Cold War adversaries was a no-no. Both embassies sent out rules of comportment to its people, but as a Fulbrighter I was in a grey area: not a diplomat, but benefiting from a U.S. government fellowship. Nobody much cared in this exotic setting, we might as well have been in an international space station circling Venus.

One week, rumors circulated that Misha's wife Natasha had been mugged in the streets of Poto-Poto. At the next meeting, I told him I'd heard, and was sorry this had happened. The wall between us fell that very instant, and we became friends almost from that moment. Neither Misha nor I really gave a damn about Afghanistan. Language was our agenda.

Though the Soviet embassy kept much closer tabs on its citizens in country than the American one did, Misha invited me over to have drinks with his Natasha. I agreed. I knew they were under a tight embassy leash.

When I met Natasha I was struck by her Slavic beauty, her humor, irony, erudition, and generosity. She taught English to anyone at the Soviet Embassy who wanted to learn. For me, the guest,
all stops out. They drew the blinds shut while I was in their little
flat, having tea and getting to know them. I was guessing they took
some risk in having me there, and I found it touching. We laughed,
told stories, and compared impressions of the harmless but stag-
nating little Congo. Natasha's English was flawless, as was Misha's
French. So we made our way through.

I shared with them overheard comments from my little academic ghetto in Bacongo, where the neighbors said, *"Congolaise-
ment"* when things were badly managed in the city. The French, at
least, should have complained less, since they lived relatively well
on their *coopérant* salaries and generous and lengthy summer vacations. They could go for years on these arrangements, saving plenty
of money to buy their houses and flats back in France. This they
never could have done without the quid pro quo of maintaining a
vanguard of French presence in a former colony.

Natasha and Misha and I met clandestinely, since their tropical
idyll could have been taken from them in an instant, leaving them
grounded in the unwanted embrace of Mother Russia for the rest of
their days, when exploration and discovery were dear to them. The
times we had pasta in my flat, we made sure to have it happen after
dark, with Misha's moped pulled into my living room, out of view
from the KGB neighbors next to me. My repertoire of cuisine was
not vast, mainly pasta with tomato sauce, pasta with pesto, pasta
with nothing much. Once I served artichokes from the local market.
Misha in particular approached them skeptically since he'd never
seen or heard of this green matter.

We joked, told stories, sang, drank, and developed trust and
affection.

Bob, the enlightened public affairs officer at the U.S. Embassy,
was intrigued when I told him about this friendship, and invited
the three of us to his house for meals as well. Bob saw their charms
as I did, and no doubt ran the logarithms in his head about what
harm might come of these meetings. Apparently he figured, as I
did, that there was no real harm in them from our side. At worst,
Misha might install bugs in Bob's apartment, then the Sovs could
listen in on inoffensive banalities if they really wanted. And what
if they did.

One month I housesat at a residence with many rooms and a swimming pool with green water. There was a giant baobab in the yard. Cooks and cleaners were feudally attached to the property and refused to go on leave. I asked the cooks to make something vegetarian, and invited Natasha and Misha over for a meal by the pool, just the three of us.

The cook's version of "vegetarian" was ground meet broiled in chicken skins. No matter, the asparagus, foufou and wine made a fine meal. We became more at ease in the tropical setting far from world conflicts and rivalries. We understood we were in the city to expand awareness and appreciation of our respective languages and cultures, but increasingly saw it as an enlargement of everyone's view of the world, including our own. Our governments probably saw us as competitors, but we never did. The more Russian, the more English, the better.

The months crept on with heat, humidity, and frustrations. My little university amphitheater was often enough commandeered for Marxist rallies, with my harmless English sessions cancelled. The Congolese students were driven to ideological rituals, with other topics relegated to lower priorities. Misha had only a few students to start with, and the results were not brilliant in his case, either. We were conscientious and hopeful, both doing the best we could under the circumstances. During our visits together—every week or so—Natasha would ask about English points of references she had learned about in the USSR (the meaning of an ironic phrase in Jane Austin, an idiom she had run across in Jack London or Mark Twain texts approved in the Soviet Union). She hungered for the insights of a native speaker. She noted them down and never forgot any of them. Likewise, over the years following, when we maintained a lively correspondence through the mail. Her aerogrammes sometimes arrived at my address in the U.S. torn open, with stamps like "arrived damaged at Newark airport" and resealed.

March and April, 1980, were devilishly hot, and only by turning up the air conditioning to the max and reading the wintry scenes in Martin Cruz Smith's *Gorky Park* was I able to cool down.

By June it was time to leave for the States, and I had to choose between flights out on a Thursday (through Kano, Nigeria) or Saturday (through Niamey, Niger). After some fussing and hesitating, I opted for the Kano flight. It brought some emotions, since I knew I might never see Natasha and Misha again.

On short notice for my Thursday flight, I stopped at Natasha's and Misha's flat to say goodbye, but they were out. I left a scribbled note at their door, telling them of my exit plans and wishing them well.

I sat in the waiting area of Maya-Maya airport that night, checked in, baggage on the tarmac waiting for the incoming UTA flight. Everything was delayed, with public address announcements to the effect of *"départ bientot"* and *"départ immédiat"* and *"départ imminent,"* all untrue as we hundred passengers sat staring into space.

A commotion stirred as two Russians broke through the forbidden tarmac perimeter and into the waiting area of the terminal. Natasha and Misha had seen my note and made their way to the most public of settings to smother me in hugs, kisses, and good wishes. A hundred passengers looked on as the scene unfolded. Anyone there could have ratted on them, resulting in permanent grounding for Misha and Natasha. Nothing involving being lined up against a wall and shot as in the older times, but certainly doom for their future travels and promotions. And all for friendship. But those hundred people kept the story to themselves.

We sat together for an hour, joking and remembering idioms and talking for all to hear, about the future of friendships in general and ours, in particular. Little did any of us know at the time, that they would be among the first chosen six years later, for a high school teachers' exchange that would take them to Wisconsin. The Cold War was loosening a bit, after the Korean Air Lines incident of 1983. So the unlikely friendship went far into the future, and continues now by phone, with the surviving Natasha after Misha's death by household accident in 2016.

The Chinese
(Skin in the Game)

February 12, 1981, Chinese instructor Dong Tieng in the language department came to me and suggested we meet at my living quarters in the Congolese-supplied professors' quarter in Bacongo, near Makélékélé. It was sort of obvious his embassy had either put him up to it, or given him special permission to venture into what must have seemed mysterious from the Chinese compound. I welcomed him over one afternoon for tea and snacks. Dong Tieng spoke no English, but his French was good enough for us to talk.

I admired his cheery openness. As he came through the door to my little apartment, he said pretty abruptly, "So, how much do they pay you?" As I remember it, this came even before his perfunctory *"bonjour."*

We figured out that for every Frenchman, the American was paid half; for every American, the Congolese counterpart earned half; and the Chinese earned only half of what the Congolese were paid. That didn't leave much for the Chinese.

Back in the day when Chinese per capita income was far lower than that their African counterparts, the Chinese were in for the long haul, and kept my colleague in country for two years, lacking the funds to get him home to China for the summer, or to get his wife a plane ticket to join him in Brazzaville. He had four students. Of the four, one made it to class occasionally, and none learned Chinese. I asked him about his students. He looked around first, lowered his voice, and said, *"paresseux* (lazy)."

"So how does the grading work?" I asked. Dong Tieng said the students would show up at exam time without any notion of how the language worked, and sat as if for a lottery on the rare chance that they might answer some of the questions correctly by guessing. This was not an ideal pedagogical setting, but as stated, China was in for the long haul. I pitied but admired my colleague.

In fact, he was pretty demoralized since he taught only the most basic language skills, basically in an empty room. I asked him about the experimental agricultural plot at the outskirts of town—painstakingly developed by Chinese aid workers, then abandoned and overgrown with weeds once it was turned over to the local ministry. He winced with disappointment and said his colleagues at the Chinese Embassy felt the same.

We found familiarity in our attachment to the four seasons of the northern hemisphere—he waxed lyrical over the blooming of the flowers in spring in Shanghai. We also shared cultures which did not favor large families, and were taken aback at the many children in Congo, in families who couldn't really afford them. An obedient follower of the one-child policy, he found the crowds in Shanghai confining.

There were contrasts, of course. I had come to Congo voluntarily, Dong Tieng had been directed to do so, drawing his tiny salary from the University of Shanghai where he normally taught his country's literature.

Dong lived in a small house with five other Chinese professors at the university. He had a bedroom for himself, other parts of the house shared. The house had a Chinese cook brought from PRC, but a Congolese driver. The five were confined to the house except on rare occasions when the supervisor approved a group sortie to see a play or sports event.

"How is it being in the Chinese expat community?" I asked.

"Too many of us!" he said. Add the professors to the many at the Chinese Embassy.

He pulled out a collection of Chinese postage stamps, some more colorful than others. He handed them over to me with a cheery generosity. I was taken aback, since it seemed this might be a rare example of something of some commercial value, from someone who might have none other. I wondered how I could ever reciprocate such kindness. I didn't have American stamps or anything much else to offer. We stayed friendly for the rest of the time that year, though he was under such scrutiny that I never again saw him socially. I'm thinking he was never punished for this adventure to alien territory, nor was he encouraged to do any more of it.

At the time of this writing, hand-wringing Africa experts in America talk of "China in Africa," as if it were something like Ebola. Seeking ways of "combating" Chinese "inroads" is a little like complaining about an umpire's call in a game where your team never made it to the ball field.

In the 1990s, Administrator Brian Atwood astutely retooled his U.S. Agency for International Development to something called "democracy," thus saving it from death at the hands of North Carolina Senator Jesse Helms. It gave a stay of execution for the Agency, but left nothing much on the ground for archaeologists to find centuries from now. Prior to the Helms aggression, AID had built air strips, agriculture plots, latrines, schools, and other things people sat up and noticed in developing countries. Atwood's Pyrrhic victory of the 1990s generated conferences, training, so-called good governance seminars and sermons, and manuals on straight book-keeping for public servants. U.S. policy didn't much back this up with penalties or rewards for the players, or tangible results. But it kept the funds moving just to keep an agency alive while under assault.

Not more or less moral and ethical than other outsiders positioning themselves at different times in Africa, the Chinese were dirt poor in the 1970s and 80s. The China of Mao took the long view, following three millennia of recorded experience and probably the first humans to codify *strategy* beyond a family or village level. Communism did not entirely turn away from Confucianism and in some ways closely shadowed it, for example putting merchants at the bottom of the social hierarchy. With that, the sum total of my anecdotal understanding of their vast civilization.

Meanwhile in Mali, the government hoped to develop rice production in the northern part of their country. Protocol demanded they direct their request first to the French. The French informed them that they saw no potential there.

Then the Mali's government turned to the donor they really wanted to engage with—the Americans. The U.S. government sent agronomists, economists, development experts, sophisticated laboratory equipment, and spent a million dollars in the 1970s to test the hypothesis.

Bad news; the Americans determined that the soil in the north of Mali was not suited to rice production, something about salinity, and so sorry.

Then the Malians asked the Chinese, the original rice people, the same question. The Chinese government said, "No idea. Let's just try."

And soon rice production flourished in the north of Mali. There you have it.

They did other admirable things in Brazzaville. Remember the barefoot doctors of twentieth-century practice? I knew an Irish writer in Brazzaville who had received an anti-malarial shot in the buttocks administered by French nuns. Well meaning, the nuns would sometimes hit the sciatic nerve and leave the patient handicapped as the leg atrophied. In the Brazzaville of 1980, I would say that about one out of ten of the citizens dragged around at least one atrophied leg—usually the left one—very incapacitated, and likely from these well-intentioned flubs.

Malachai told me he'd been severely affected by this misfortune, and that acupuncture by a Chinese barefoot doctor had not only saved his leg, but over a lengthy treatment got it back to its full, original state. Malachai was a confident sort of fellow and walked with brisk strides. He owed it all to the Chinese.

Fast forward to 2018, and we see a city transformed, largely from Chinese engineering and investment. No doubt the donors have seen far-reaching advantages to themselves, and work hard in the Congo not from love for the Congolese. But you have to admit, they are engaged. They have changed the cityscape of Brazzaville with their purposeless but impressive bridge to nowhere (*"Bonne Année"* and *"Joyeux Noël"* emblazoned in lights among the filigreed wires of the suspension structure). They have paved the adjoining *corniche* which gives the river's edge a character of bold and optimistic advancement which was sadly lacking before. None of this was done to improve the daily lives of the inhabitants, but sometimes people just build as they can, and deserve credit for it.

China now reaps a harvest from its earlier plantings. Granted, entirely for itself. At least they have marked the landscape and built football stadiums to respond to a population's hunger for public spectacle. These very structures can sometimes be used for unintended evil purposes later (viz., the massacre in the stadium in Conakry, Guinea, in 2009). You can win or lose by rolling the dice. But by not rolling them at all, you guarantee the outcome to be nothing.

Congolese students in 2018 told me they had seen Chinese workers in the littoral of the country working on a new railroad to the coast. They were loading containers with *dirt* for export to China. Dirt is not exactly petroleum or diamonds, and I don't suppose there are regulations against "stealing" it. It seems the topsoil in China is depleted in some areas, after millennia of agriculture. Congo will one day regret the resources lost to outside exploitation, but then, this would be the same disappointment they have had ever since the colonial era, then the Cold War, which brought them nothing much.

America and the EU could continue to grouse about Chinese exploitation in third world countries, but only the grousers' timidity and lack of entrepreneurial spirit stop them from stepping in with something better. They note Chinese "predatory" lending practices, and compare them to a "Friday loan sharks" tantalizing vulnerable, low-salaried workers high interest rates to get them through the weekend.

An alternative would be to come up with fresh capital and infrastructure at better rates.

The Dogs

About 15,000 years ago, humans figured out how to domesticate wolves, favor their dog-like qualities in breeding, and call them "dogs" or whatever the word was back then. That's pretty recent, if you figure humans have been around for maybe 300,000 years. Dogs provide amusement and affection of course, but also potentially protection, companionship of last resort, lessons in ethics. By which I mean, they demonstrate shifting priorities between food and friendship where the one has to prevail over the other. Cats will leave you and look for something better; dogs usually won't. In fact, as humans got to rely on them for their sound advice and approval, they unwittingly made the dogs dependent on them as well. Some were tossed back into the wild, and became "feral."

Cultures incorporate dogs one way or another. It tells something about peoples' values to observe to what extent they are encouraged to mingle with us. In some places they are taken as members of the family.

Feral or stray dogs are nearly everywhere. Being one of these unfortunate creatures can be tolerable, bad, worse, or horrible, depending on where destiny has left them.

In 1979-81 in Brazzaville, dogs were either big lottery winners or losers. The groomed and bred ones, many of them immense and cherished in the French expatriate houses they lived in, ate many times more meat daily than an average Congolese family of six. Like bulls bred for the bullfight, they were pampered and adored until the time of reckoning came. For the bull, an hour of stress and torment, then a death considered noble and enviable by aficionados of the sport. For the pampered dogs in Congo, a fate far worse: abandonment in the uncaring streets of Brazzaville when the time came for summer vacation in France. I don't know if the expats premeditated these cruel deceptions, but you could see the bewilderment of these helpless animals left behind.

In a few cases we left food out for them and included them in our academic ghetto—the French neighbor, the Iranian, the Brit, the Italian, myself. But we knew that we, too, would leave one day. We discussed the morality of prolonging and delaying the agony of these harmless animals well born, now feral. None of us had the means to get a dog through quarantine, let alone give it basic support, back in our home countries. We cursed the French who did this, but then, the kind and caring Ange next door was also French.

The losers by far were the local strays, whose entire lives were marked by privation, torment, anxiety, and gloom.

In 1981 after my return to the country, I had no housing when the Congolese government failed with their end of the bargain to give me a place to live. The U.S. embassy kindly found temporary remedies. One of my way stations was the residence of the absent deputy chief of mission, who was away in the States for her annual leave. I house sat for her, and was told to go easy on the cook and gardener and housekeeper, and only to make sure the dog was fed. These three loyal staff members looked with amazement as they themselves did their twice-daily feedings of the massive German shepherd, piling mountains of meat on a large plate at midday and late afternoon. The staff knew that a single serving of that dog's rations would have fed their families for a month. They would sometimes look at me in puzzlement. I could only shrug and express my amazement as well, but I don't know if they ever believed me.

Islam has mixed reviews on dogs, making it *haraam* to snuggle too closely or abide their saliva, though not to own them. Though "dog" can be part of a Middle Eastern curse, it is acceptable to have them around, not acceptable to keep them on a short leash for long periods of time, or show other forms of cruelty. In most cases religious beliefs are otherwise indifferent to the pros and cons of having dogs around. They leave the human side of it up to the individual. Here we observe the levels of empathy, cruelty, indifference, affection that come up in different cultures, which in fact are reflected in how individuals treat their dogs.

Hitler had a dog and probably was a vegetarian. Spain's Franco, though, hated them (the feral kind) and ordered all strays eliminated in a massive caninocide in the 1950s-60s. To this day, you won't find any in Spain, at least not in the major cities.

In Mexico, people show unprovoked cruelty, kicking and tormenting them when mere neglect could do just as well. I've witnessed this pretty uniformly in Mexico City and Cuernavaca, though admittedly some decades ago. It's possible that in a culture of privation and injustice, the more unfortunate people in society get to demonstrate that there are sentient beings beneath them. As societies advance materially, dogs usually get a pass, then sometimes a place of honor.

The French bring them into restaurants to be by their side during a meal, as they would their children. This implies something more than acceptance, though the feral variety can get harsh treatment as well. Lacking a language we are smart enough to follow, the dogs likely wonder how offspring from the same litter could be so exalted and so despised. Philosophers among dogs (especially the little bearded ones with inquisitive eyes) have debated his question through the ages. Certainly the French ones, which are existentialists.

In La Fontaine's autobiographical fable, the famished wolf approaches his cousin, the dog, content to eat at its bowl. The dog explains that the deal is favorable: he feigns affection for the master, and in return gets regular meals and humane treatment. He invites his cousin the wolf to give it a try. The wolf is tempted. Then with a start, it sees the leash around the dog's neck, asks, "What is that?!" When he finds out, makes a break for it, cannot get far enough away, and "is still running to this day."

In some Asian countries dogs are raised for food. This seems inhumane to Westerners, who nevertheless torture newborn calves to call them "veal." What happens at slaughterhouses in Western countries will turn any visitor into a vegetarian. I am saying this only to disqualify cultures from condemning others, though there may be some objective and universal standards we may one day attain. Even the notable and much regretted Anthony Bourdain noted the cruelty and gore in his 1999 *New Yorker* article, "Don't eat before reading this."

In America, dogs get shots, pedigrees, expensive gourmet food, solemn funerals, bubble baths, psychiatrists, mood enhancers, even organ replacement. We know future anthropologists/ archeologists will determine that Americans worshipped dogs and clocks, which appear on the facades of its banks, aka temples. They may lump us in with Mayas and some traditional Oceanic peoples as having beliefs that are just plain inexplicable.

Sweden's Lasse Hallström made a haunting film in 1985 called *My Life as a Dog*. It showed a twelve-year-old philosopher consumed by life's imponderables, as any twelve-year-old is. Set in 1958 during the early years of Soviet space exploration, the film shows the boy, Ingmar, anguished by the needless cruelty of sending of a dog, Laika, into space and leaving her there to starve. Stunned by the injustice of it and by his own powerlessness in general, Ingmar transforms himself into a higher being: he becomes Laika herself, barking at family members when he sees the futility of arguing or defending himself among them. His kinship with a four-legged he has never met, but heard about, becomes the one certainty in his unmoored life.

Huskies in Arctic regions are the willing saviors of humans stuck in those inhospitable climes.

In Mongolia, nomadic herders developed the Bankhar breed over the centuries, to protect their livestock from predators. Soviet occupation almost rooted them out, but now they are making a comeback.

In the Grimms' fairy tale, "The Dog and the Sparrow," the dog's only true friend, the sparrow, gets justice when a carter with horse and wagon willfully runs over the sleeping dog in a ditch. The sparrow renders Job-like punishment on the carter for his careless disregard. Remember, of course, how Grimms' tales were teaching devices to inculcate ethics and morality.

Chekhov's 1899 story "The Lady and the Little Dog" tells how marital infidelity in Yalta could happen thanks to a small dog furnishing the channel through which Dmitri Gurov and Anna Sergeyevna could meet and carry on. Anna meant to say, "Come hither," but couldn't ever have carried it through without the dog's help.

The urinating puppies in Tintoretto's Nativity scenes remind us that daily life was made more human with the accompaniment of the four-leggeds. Likewise, in Velázquez's masterwork *Las Meninas*, an astonished mastiff takes a central role in the enigmatic painting.

Certainly dogs have sharp memories (*viz.* Argos in the *Odyssey*, the only member of the household to get an immediate fix on Odysseus's identity when the latter returns to Ithaca after ten years of war). They may even have oral traditions passed on through the generations, which a future argologist or arfologist may figure out how to decipher.

Fast forward to 2018 in Brazzaville, no pampered French dogs at all, and from the few visits I was able to make to Congolese and expats' homes, I never saw a dog in a home. But I couldn't help see the presence nearly everywhere of an appealing breed of strays. They were smallish, entirely unaggressive, and all had similar coloring, a mottled brown or tan. Their Adam and Eve were constructed for efficiency and modesty of need. They hoped for everything, expected nothing, in keeping with what human philosophers have always advised. They never made eye contact—not from fear, so much as from resignation that nothing would ever come of it.

With the people in my neighborhood, the dogs coexisted in harmony and yet never any interaction. The latter had little choice but to hang around the humans especially at meal time. The humans put up no opposition or cruelty, nor did they "care for" the dogs or ever lead them to expect treats. What fell off the table was fair game, though it was never enough to make a meal. All these likeable creatures were tortured with fleas and other parasites, and spent their lives trying to bite them out of their fur. What might they have known of soaps and baths and treatments for these conditions? Humans rightly went guiltless for neglecting these cures, since they themselves had no extra resources to spend, and suffered from their own itching.

The Congolese showed no meanness, neither did they have much interest in these unfortunates, or take it upon themselves to improve their plight. They had their own challenges.

As I took my morning walk from my borrowed house to the embassy, I went through these decent but spare quarters. People and dogs both took notice of me very quickly. When the infants greeted me with gentle waves of their tiny hands, I waved back and the neighbors smiled and sometimes even greeted me themselves. In the hierarchy of needs and resources, it was pretty clear I was the lucky one, with the neighbors a close second and the strays a distant third. As I tried to take pictures with my iPad without being noticed, of course everyone saw me in an instant and arranged themselves in case I should want to get them in that shot. Quickly they figured out it was really the dogs I was after. They knew that I knew that they knew that I knew that no one in this scenario could alter the imbalance. They took no comfort or sense of superiority of the dogs amongst them, but nor could they draw down on the rationed shares of compassion they had to save for their own offspring. I liked my neighbors a lot.

Whimpering is a luxury only for creatures with expectations. Brazzaville's dogs knew better. They sought the cooler temperatures of the shade and accommodated themselves to parasites, heat, undernourishment, and their pointless existence. Yet they were fully part of the scene. I never saw a human shoo away or kick at a canine.

Anyone would want to rescue them all. But to be realistic, in circumstances none of them really chose, you would have to do triage. By this reckoning, humans had to come first, and too bad for the losers.

Other Members of the Animal Kingdom

The fauna and flora also give the place character.

Tropical zones are bountiful in providing geckos as entertainment. Their simplest sketch is the pushups they do to develop their abs. This may seem a simple matter, but their trainers have them taking starting positions vertically on a wall or even suspended from ceilings. Circus animals develop routines over months; the geckos spring into their advanced techniques from birth or hatchment. As quick studies, they are unsurpassed. They wear tiny earpods to keep them in rhythm during their workouts, piping in gecko cantatas and sometimes a langorous fado of their forbears. When excited, they speed up their workouts to a fevered pitch, I think as exhibitionists. Their performances seem contrived for the humans, they can't have much utility otherwise. I've never seen a gecko performing when I wasn't watching, so I don't know for sure.

Though their stage routines may have to do with hunting and mating, it seems their gyrations are mainly for show. They aren't only harmless to humans, they're also harmful to humans' annoyances such as buzzing insects and mites too small to see but large enough to annoy. I see them as benign. I would leave cheese out for them, little grains or whatever. But it seems they are independent and also indifferent to our offerings. I don't know about their life spans or life expectancy, but they seem to live fulfilling lives, at least amusing ones.

They are funnier than Saturday Night Live, more informative than Meet the Press.

In Brazzaville they chased along the walls, catching insects too small for the human eye to see, then pursuing one another most comically. They surely had some reproductive routines, but did them not only with heels and backwards, but with suction cups on their tiny feet to do what they did vertically suspended. I never saw a Ginger Rogers gecko actually taken by a Fred Astaire one, but maybe they reserved those moments for private showings only, or pay-per-view. It is one of nature's most generous freebees, and you're welcome.

Tarantulas on the other hand are creepy, even though in fact they may be as harmless as geckos, I don't know. One was living under my refrigerator in my Bacongo flat. I think if it considered itself helpful or harmless, it would have come out into the open. But it must have known how bad it looked. Lurking in the dark shades of the nether refrigerator region, it seemed either frightened or guilty. Maybe the shame of its ugliness drove it into hiding. It was the size of a Maryland crab, but grew in the imagination to Maine lobster size if you figured in its horrible furry legs.

One day I found it reaching out from beneath its hiding place, and it made me cry. Not from fear really, but just from having to share my living quarters with an eight-legged so massive. I would have negotiated a truce if I could have known what it was looking for, and would have left some of that for it outside. I would have asked for services in exchange, possibly an agreement to pursue and devour lesser pests streaming into the house at all hours. Maybe my tarantula might have taken an offer of cooperation and non-aggression, but our languages didn't overlap. No need to explain in detail how this beast was banished from my kitchen, but let's just say I was as tolerant as I could be before turning to harsh methods of elimination.

Now, the *fourous*. *Fourous* are a sort of stealth fly, light enough to go unnoticed, rarely seen, and the source of horrible agony for dogs and people. You will almost never see them, but when they get what they need from your ankle or neck or wrists, they excite murderous passions. They take infinitesimal doses of blood, the little vampires. They are more skillful than a lab nurse in finding an untapped blood vessel and its capillaries. They are post doc level microbiologists. They never put their knowledge to any use or benefit to anyone. Any normal person would cry out to them, "Just tell me where to leave it, and I'll give you some cc's of blood to you, no questions asked." But the *fourous* don't negotiate. Their hateful little existences have no merit to anyone other than themselves.

I knew a gentle soul at the U.S. Embassy, whose ancestors were victims of intimidation, humiliation and murder. He fancied the only reasonable action toward *fourous*: exterminate them! Sometimes in objectifying our enemies and dehumanizing them, we approach their real essence. If genocide is the process of imagining the enemy as worthless annoyances, *fourous* would be the perfect example. They may have sneaked onto Noah's ark, but the point is made. Noah's scheme was as imperfect as all others. As they are now configured, *fourous* surely should be lined up against a wall, a stick-em on their frenzied, vile little hearts now targets, given a last cigarette and blindfold, and then blam and to hell with them.

It may be anthropomorphic to think this way, but sometimes you just have to take sides.

Between the charm and benefits provided by geckos, to the affliction of *fourous* especially at sunset, the gamut is wide between the creatures we appreciate and those we don't. Like other predators, we, too, have the ability to slay those we despise, and favor those we don't. Just don't exterminate them all, because for some of our allies they look like food. Probably there's a Greater Balance we'll never understand.

If North America has growing populations of stink bugs which came as hitchhikers on airplanes from Asia, then Brazzaville had its own variety of snakes, insects, arthropods, flyers, swimmers, creepers, slimers, terrified mammals, pests and friends to adapt to. A tolerant spirit and the occasional brachypemocide carried us through, and affirmed us as but one player in nature's restless struggles.

Journal Entries, 1981

Wednesday, March 11
Bravo for the Congolese government, which yesterday reinstated the private soccer clubs. It had outlawed them months ago, as tribalist and primitive. A government which can admit its mistakes has much in its favor....

Tuesday, March 31
Ange and Arounothay went out in Ange's handsome, home-made pirogue, only to be nearly killed by a hippo they unwittingly disturbed in the Djoué. Arounothay says he is cured of ever wanting to go boating again; Ange, too embarrassed to mention the incident himself. The pirogue he has gouged out over the months remains in his front yard, not to be used again

...Gabriel says my house has been "blessed," perhaps by a French priest by the name of Bernard, who Gabriel maintains could pass for my grandfather, and who used to pray in the house. In fact, my flat has been harmonious, in contrast to the Pétra/Natat building next door. Pétra is *"gentille,"* says Gabriel, "but his *gentillesse* ends up being mean."

Gabriel says the nation has had only one real president: the Abbé Youlou. There were no regional factions under Youlou, and everything we can see in the country is his doing. When the soldiers have finished killing off one another, he says, there will be a second real president, and then the country can pick up where it left off....

A student says to me, "You'll see. At the first opportunity, the day it becomes possible, every African country where there are any Soviets, will kick them out in a minute. As for now, they can't. They're too afraid."

Saturday, April 4
An ugly scene between Gabriel and his boss Ange, over something to do with the hedge. A year of accumulated disgust has welled up in Gabriel, who will now probably leave, pending how Natat may intervene in the affair. Gabriel keeps repeating, "I've never seen such a thing as the way Pétra spoke to Natat last fall." Delphine and the three children drifted around during the dispute, not knowing where to go or hide. I had them all in for tonic while working on Gabriel to join us and calm down and vent his rage. Later he re-

peated to me, as the other day: "You see? I told you your house was blessed."

…Meanwhile to complete the Goldoni neighborhood scene, an antic chase scene by the Harrisons, trying to pull back their dog Spotty from the Soviets' yard for the fortieth time, where he has an obsessive predilection to go wherever he's loose. The Soviets assume they're suspected of something, raise their hands in defense. *"Mais ce n'est pas nous qui l'appelons!"*

…And finally, Natasha and Misha. Mid-morning meal with them today. I went to deliver records I'd gotten for them in the U.S. on spring break, and they awaited with an unexpected large meal, 10:00 a.m. "It's not every day that someone comes to visit us," they said.

This may be a rare time this year of the Soviet invasion of Afghanistan that an American has broken bread with Soviets, certainly in Brazzaville; the three of us felt a sense of pent-up yearning to overcome barriers.

First, laughter over drinking vodka at 10:00 in the morning. "This is a day for breaking rules," said Misha's wife Natasha, whom I've just met for the first time. We learn about one another. Misha is from a region in USSR with one hundred ethnic groups, with no idea of his own provenance. Natasha, though a Cossack, is afraid to climb onto a moped let alone a horse; their secret longings (to see California); their fears that war will break out between our two countries, the degree to which they are monitored ("No, they wouldn't mind if we came over to see you. At least, I…don't… think… so.")

We ate smoked fish wrapped in a page of *Pravda* with a cartoon of the U.S. driving a tank into El Salvador. "Vietnam, Afghanistan?" Natasha said, "I don't think the two are quite similar. But victims are victims."

We ended up exchanging gifts, laughing over all the rules we'd just broken, and making a tentative date to see a movie together next week.

A hope: to see their Russia one day, and show them my America.

Sunday, April 12
Children are disappearing in Bacongo, rumored to be murdered and decapitated. People say some think their brains might harbor diamonds, something like oysters developing pearls. Just rumors.

A guided tour through UNDP Bernard Rivaillon's apartment, where I was shown bullet holes from a previous coup. Talk of another one in the summer, to displace Congolese officials not loyal enough to Marxism-Leninism.

An Englishman and a Soviet died last week in Pointe Noire, of malaria.

Saw *One Flew over the Cuckoo's Nest* with Natasha and Misha, who loved it.

Today, met an American courier of sensitive materials from Washington to the embassies. He says he does ten missions a year, and about 250,000 miles. That is pretty much the distance to the moon.

Wednesday, April 22
Natasha and Misha asked to see my unpublished novels, what they call "American *samizdat.*" Misha says his one hundred students at the university will never get to travel to the USSR, thus making his job "meaningless."

...Proliferation of demagogic holidays, seminars, rallies, marking the premature end of the academic calendar. This week it's the *semaine culturelle*, with rallies and *soirées dansantes* by the Jeunesse pour l'anti-imperialism. Next week they will celebrate the anniversary of changing the university's name. The following week is workers' day, May 1. I've told my students I will offer classes on any of these official days, and won't blame any for respecting whatever holiday they feel they must. Classes, though, are suspended and forbidden.

Sunday, April 26
　　Q. What is capitalism?
　　A. Man's inhumanity to man.
　　Q. What is communism?
　　A. The reverse.

Monday, May 18
President Sassou's spokesman was to accompany Sassou on a trip to Moscow, meanwhile the spokesman had been invited to a conference in Syracuse, New York, at a conflicting time. He asked his boss what he should do. Despite the importance of the trip to Moscow, Sassou is said to have told him, "It's more important you go

to the United States. Arrange your schedule however you must, to fit it in."

Sunday, May 24
With the election of François Mitterrand, the Congolese wonder out loud how Giscard would not call out the army, or why, as a deposed president, he should not be killed or put in jail.

The ants have taken over my kitchen. Something to do with the dry season. It's like an Italian short story, "The Ants."

Wednesday, May 25
Time is running out and my fondness for this place and my calm and healthy existence here grows. I'll be sad to leave, and aggressive in my appeals to be sent back again next year.

Monday, June 8
Saw *Fiddler on the Roof* with Natasha and Misha. To them, the movie smacked of current socialist realism critiques of the ancient regime, and only irritated them.

Then, a university departure dinner for me and for Dong Tieng, also departing, at a restaurant in Poto-Poto. I sat opposite Misha, and people kept joking about and applauding our teasing of each other. It seems our Congolese colleagues' impression of the three of us is our ability to poke fun. People remarked the moment including Soviets, Irish, English, Americans, Laotians, an Iranian, Congolese all getting along.

Then, my departure: Natasha and Misha appear before me at the airport waiting area, making their way in from forbidden areas of the airport tarmac to say goodbye.

They risked much in making their way over to me in front of a crowd. The crowd observed the naughtiness of our unlikely friendship, but no gossip or comments. Natasha and Misha and I fell into one another's arms, then I boarded the plane and left.

Departing

Finally, it was time to wend my way home from this enriching year-and-a-half. All flights stopped somewhere on the way to Paris, so I chose the UTA itinerary which landed in Kano, Nigeria, at 3:00 a.m. for refueling.

I had a prior history with Kano, but had never been there. In 1979 I'd gotten word that the university there, Ahmadou Bello, had sought me out to offer me a job in its French department. I'd heard about this in January of that year, from friends in Boston and Providence who had left cryptic messages to this effect. I was ready to go. I packed my bags and waited for further news.

A long silence followed, and I tried sending telegrams, aerogrammes, and phone calls to the French department at Ahmadou Bello. No response. I would have decamped to the town in northern Nigeria, but had no information on the time or place I was supposed to show up.

Three months later, in March, I received a letter by international post, dated January 10, summoning me to an interview on campus for two days later, January 12. It said, "Your interview is tomorrow. Kindly do not be late." This seemed either fate's intervention, or possibly ridicule or incompetence on the part of the university there.

Now as I departed Brazzaville with mixed feelings, I looked forward to the chance to breathe in the Kano air and sense the path not taken, even at 3:00 a.m. when the northern Nigerian heat would be at its lowest point of the day.

On the Brazzaville-Kano leg of the flight, I pondered the events and circumstances which had brought me to this point:

Nineteen seventy-three, I had first ventures to Africa on a tourist air ticket, misled by an arithmetic error to believe I had two thousand dollars in the bank, when in fact there was only $1000. I'd gone into a travel agency whose marquee said "Please go away." I asked for the next flight to Africa. Nonplussed, they found a flight to Casablanca the same week, one of the few countries on the Continent that didn't require visas for Americans. I took it, then found the Senegal and Mali consulates in Casablanca and arranged for visits to those two countries. The Casablanca-Dakar-Bamako circuit cost me one thousand dollars US, hotels and expenses included, and this resulted in my introductory trip to Sub-Saharan Africa and my discovery of this world, its charms, its presence in my future wanderings. But for my fortunate $1000 arithmetic error, I never would have discovered this world of challenge and discovery.

Taking me from Casablanca to Dakar in 1973, the plane banked towards its landing, and flew low over the lands adjoining the Dakar destination. From the airplane window I saw a goat herder looking up to the plane and, I believed, establishing eye contact with me in the plane. "What is your purpose in coming here?" the goatherd seemed to say to me, with a skeptical glance.

I thought back to an African's account, during my interpreting days: "The lady on the Paris Metro said judgmentally, *"Jeune homme, dans notre pays on donne la place aux agées."* (In our country, people give up their seats to an older lady.")

"Ah, bon?" had been the African's response. "In my country we eat them."

On my way back home going through Kano, I remembered the heroic days of thirty-five millimeter projectors bringing American films to remote African villages, showing the entertainments outdoors on bistro walls during the clear Sahel nights. I never learned to thread these projectors myself, but had seen the audiences reacting to scenes of note, especially the love scenes which drew sighs, whistles, and approving comments. *West Side Story*, the *Ten Commandments* were powerful inspirations for African audiences starved of information and drama. They loved those experiences and piled loud approbation for fictions which fed their imaginations.

I remembered my "yellow meals" —dinners I made of maize, papaya, spaghetti, mango, eggs, pineapple, and couscous. Monotonous though they were, they nourished and encouraged investigation and study.

I remembered my second year in the city, when I received worthless ministry chits for hotel rooms in government-owned hotels. The hotels declined my coupons disdainfully, saying, "The government never backs these IOUs with any payments. Sorry but can't give you a room here."

I had invited the Harrisons, so erratic, so generous to me in their many meals and permissions to use their phone for incoming international calls. I'd taken them to a local establishment to return in kind their many acts of hospitality. The sole menu item that day had been monkey brain stew, which the Harrisons ate gratefully. I said to the owners, "You've got to have some eggs back there some-where, somehow. Now get me some of them."

Having none in the kitchen, they went out to the local market to buy some and make omelets for me.

I remembered the Brazzaville zoo, that dreadful holding house for primates locked up without habeas corpus. The gorilla had reached out its bony hand to me as I passed in front, as if to say, "Why am I here?"

I remembered the stray Soviet women, shuffling along the back roads of the capital and begging for alms, after marrying Congolese students who had been to Moscow, then returned and abandoned their young wives. Too poor to care for their compatriots, the Soviets had left these women to fend for themselves. Their begging and alms never added up to a ticket home to Moscow, so they became fixtures in Brazzaville's desperate street culture. Living in misery, they made up a small European proletariat in the Congo capital.

I remembered the generosity of the Pushkin Institute, who had welcomed me to their afternoon language classes, and showered me with gifts the day I stopped in to say goodbye. Records, books, chocolates piled on the desk of the registrar who had been expecting my farewell visit. I had so little to reciprocate, only a picture book of America's natural parks.

I remembered the slatted windows in my university flat, hero-ically omitting screens or other ways of keeping mosquitoes out of the house. Had the French builders seen screenless windows as a sort of manly defiance of malaria?

I remembered the spigots gone dry, the lack of water not three hundred meters from the world's swiftest flowing river.

These thoughts occupied and distracted me during the five-hour transit from Brazzaville to Kano.

Once in the Kano airport I decided to get off the plane during the one-hour layover and refueling. Why not breathe, just once, the air of the city I might have known and inhabited if things had gone differently?

I asked the flight crew for a transit tag, but they'd run out. They assured me I could get back on the plane an hour later, no prob-lem. I walked off the huge plane and over to the only destination in the area, a small guard house which served as departure lounge and customs facility for the northern Nigerian airport in the darkest heat of the northern Sahelian night.

I entered the guard house, where an armed Nigerian customs official demanded to see my papers. "I left them on the plane. I'm a transit passenger," I said, pointing at the airplane out on the tarmac.

"You are now on Nigerian soil," the customs official said menacingly. "You will show your papers." He fingered the holstered pistol at his waist. I reached for my wallet, and this only antagonized him more. He wanted to assert authority, not take a bribe. On the instructions of the flight crew, I'd left my passport and air ticket on my seat in the plane.

I saw this was going badly. I looked at my choices: Defy the constabulary and take my chances getting back to the plane. Or submit to him and be taken to a local holding cell, miss the takeoff and risk getting dysentery in my three-day ordeal in a Nigerian prison. I decided dysentery might be worse than death, so I planned to make a run for it to the airplane and hope for the best.

I explained in French to the French passenger in the same predicament, "I am going to count to three then we will run toward the airplane. I doubt if they would kill both of us," I said. "*D'accord*," said my French counterpart who had his own woes and was imagining his own doomsday scenarios.

I counted to three, and the Frenchman and I bolted from the customs shack toward the plane. The customs official took out his pistol from his holster, running behind to try to catch us. He aimed but didn't fire his weapon, so I am alive now to tell the story.

Two

The River and its Basin

The River

For nineteenth-century European explorers, the Congo was their Everest, their Mars, and Holy Grail.

It wasn't the only one, since pre-spatial orbit geographers weren't sure about the source of the Nile. Livingston, Stanley, Brazza, Richard Burton, Mungo Park, John Speke, and others went from compulsion, ambition, curiosity, their claustrophobia in the northern European cities they hailed from. They went with backing from science foundations, governments, the newly emerging mass media, and sponsors like King Leopold II of Belgium.

Add greed to the list of motivators. Driven by wanderlust and maybe guilt from their intrusions and destructions of exotic civilizations, the explorers took with them a faraway gaze mixing disgust for the tedium of their homes, a yearning for distance and discovery, reckless domination, conquest. These were not "naturists." They sought a sort of immortality, and achieved it to a degree, in fame alone. Many filed reports, studies, newspaper dispatches, and kept diaries and chronicles. Enamored of record keeping, they were in a sense the first historiographers of the African Continent, in the shadow of their antecedent Herodotus in 350 BCE. The latter was curious, too, about the source of the Nile, but didn't have the geographic girth of those who benefited from steamships, supplies bundled for the long haul, or merchants preceding them, and scratching the surface of lands mainly for the plunder they served up.

Of the long and sorry lists of human cruelties and sadism, not many exceed the cynicism of Leopold II of Belgium, who took lands he never visited or even saw, comprising a surface about equal in size to modern Europe, and making them into his personal property. The Congo Free State is chronicled by Mark Twain (*King Leopold's Soliloquy,* 1905) and others, including the horrifying *King Leopold's Ghost* by Adam Hochschild, 1999.

V.S. Naipaul's *Bend in the River,* 1979, a more recent account echoing Conrad's *Heart of Darkness,* 1899, established a standard of depravity which leached into the character of the instigators. But from where? The Conrad-Naipaul model demonstrated the flowering of sinister impulses rather on those who seized the loot, linking them in some way to the innate nature of the place itself. These are of course projections by the predators of the malice they had within themselves, attributing them to outside forces putting them under some sort of spell.

We know that Francis Ford Coppola's 1979 film *Apocalypse Now* drew from the same sources, imagining that brutal conditions in non-European settings could bring out the looniest of their protagonists' natures. In fairness to the artists cited, it seems that their depictions of the harsh terrain were mainly caricatures. They meant to show that perpetrators of butchery and cruelty need look no farther their own dark souls. The harsh surroundings merely released the nastiness already implicit in their nature. We are asked to believe that Western civilization only represses but does not really root out these impulses. Fair enough, though readers and viewers inevitably have seen more clearly the settings of these works, rather than an explanation of how and why people go screwy under the challenges of displacement.

Hochschild posits that *Heart of Darkness* may not have been entirely fiction after all, and that Kurz and others in the Conrad story can be identified as certain merchants and adventurers Conrad actually met when he was in the region. The adventurers should be admired for their restless curiosity, condemned for their reckless cruelty.

The Democratic Republic of the Congo, DRC, maintains in its current form a demonstration of how large human organizations can violate and betray their own people, time and again. As I write in 2018, Laurent Kabila has ceded his presidency to the son of an opposition leader, Félix Antoine Tshilombo Tshisekedi, who is believed to have offered a sweet deal to Kabila, better than that of the real opposition winner, Martin Fayulu. Thus, the son of a genuine opposition leader entered into a bargain with the son of a previous dictator to carry on as their fathers did, only this time as allies of each other. The African Union, the Catholic Church, and the United States all questioned the outcome of the election but ultimately assented, possibly with condescension toward the people who voted otherwise.

No continent is inherently "bad" or "good," but the maneuverings in the two Congos were possible only with the complicity and cooperation of multinational organizations seeking "stability" of their supplies of diamonds, gold, copper, cobalt, tin, and coltan, the mineral needed for cell phones. All understood that the point was to assure resource supplies to industrialized countries, rather than the well-being of its citizens. Nothing new here, from the European and North American support for dictator Mobuto Sese Seko Kuku Ngbendu Wa Za Banga, 1965-97, who filled chartered Boeing jets in the 1970s with camp followers on junkets to Washington and San Francisco in search of development money for his country. All knew he took it for himself, all understood this was the quid pro quo that would move the cobalt, copper, and other treasures to those who most sought them.

In 1980 I saw the famous half-built building in Kinshasa abandoned in mid construction one day when the world market price for copper fell from four dollars per pound to below two, in a matter of a few days. An immense crane stood by its side for about a decade, both the crane and the never-completed building standing as monuments to the Devils' deals to plunderers on both sides.

If you superimpose a map of DRC on one of Europe, the country extends from Scotland to Sicily, from Aquitaine to Poland. It is large. A single game park in South Africa—Kruger—is bigger than Belgium, which seized wealth and territory in Leopold's Congo Free State. A significant accomplishment for a tiny nation, and not one which covers it in glory. One of the earliest troop movements during the Rwanda genocide of 1994 was the evacuation of Belgian troops after ten were killed at the beginning of the war. All histories have strands of shame.

The DRC I remember from 1980 ("Zaire") was unique in its vast creepiness. As if to satisfy the Western seeker of exoticism, the single way to cross the river was on "Le Beach," a chug-chug launch that seemed to be of the Joseph Conrad era. Something like a water taxi, the Beach had an unconvincing motor that evoked the early days of the steam engine. Those crossing over knew that if the engine failed, or if the fuel ran out, it would mean death as the powerful current swept them to the rapids downstream. Judging by the water lilies flowing downstream, it seemed that the current must be overpowering; the lilies floated past at thirty-five miles per hour, so it seemed. It seemed like fair warning from this gorgeous natural phenomenon, fearsome in its force and compellingly beautiful in what Michelangelo would have called *terribilità*.

The beautiful Stanley Pool is probably the widest passage in the River. Imagine something about twice the width of the Hudson, maybe more. On opposite sides, within view of each other, are the former Leopoldville—now Kinshasa—and Brazzaville. My first time over, I thought I should have a look at the other side, for context and a sense of where I was in the world. These days, visas are indispensable. No one so much cared in 1980, so long as you had a passport from some country or other. Mobutu had renamed the majestic river the "Zaire," but everyone knew it was really the Congo and always would be.

The larger country's leader had chosen capitalism as the country's system, and was BFF with the United States, Belgium, France and other Western nations. Congo-Brazzaville's leaders had chosen the other path, and aligned with the USSR in the proxy rivalries of the Cold War.

Boarding the Beach in Brazzaville was normal and even friendly back then. The arrival in Kinshasa, not so. The Zaire border police, in U.S. Army surplus uniforms and helmets, scrutinized all passengers with an eye to shaking them down, and put up all possible obstacles in entering Zaire. In my case a bad-tempered customs official waved me in, then hours later found me walking the streets of Kinshasa and hit me up for a bribe. "I was the one who let you in," he said. In Kinshasa the distinction between bribes and extortion was a thin veil. "Don't you remember me?" he said.

I said, "No," but understood I was being watched in a system that was there mainly to hassle people. The customs officer was underpaid and badly treated by his government, but I knew that I alone could not fix his problem.

I explored the streets of gloomy Kinshasa, sensing everywhere I went that people eyed me, calculating what I might have in local currency and how they might get their share of it.

A man approached me, wanting to sell me little images of local scenes, made of butterfly wings.

"*Dernier prix?*" the salesman said, pushing the merchandise at me, sort of like enlarged postcards. I knew the local protocol was to bargain and make insultingly low offers on these artisanal creations. The thing was, I had no interest at all in owning these things.

I took a second and third look at the street vendor, and realized he was *starving*. The bidding and haggling game was game only to Western visitors; for local vendors, it was life or death. It all seemed grotesque in the context of local norms of street markets, when in fact the vendors were in second and third stages of starvation.

I gave the vendor twice his asking price for an item I didn't want, realizing this was in fact his form of begging. I cursed the corrupt leaders who had left him in this predicament, and the leaders' allies and the multinationals who sealed the fate of the hoards of people under its corrupt rule. Mobutu, the Belgians, the Americans, the multinationals, all complicit in this assault on humans unlucky enough to be born in a doomed, so-called country.

I would have stayed overnight at a cheap hotel in Kinshasa, but didn't really want to spend even an hour more in this sordid situation. I took my walk, got my sandwich and Coke, and headed back to the Beach the same afternoon.

On board for the trip back to Brazzaville, one passenger lacked the proper paper to cross over to Brazzaville. Five nasty-looking officers confronted the man with rubber whips and threats. About forty passengers had a look at the scene, knowing they couldn't do anything about it.

"*Sortez!*" the officers said to the man sitting on the rear row of benches on the boat. "*Sortez, sortez!*" They took some swipes at him with their truncheons. All eyes went to this drama, curious to see the outcome. All knew a bribe or extortion would play out, and were looking for what came next.

The police circled around the undocumented passenger, but he refused to leave the vessel as it prepared for its launch to the other side of the river. "*Sortez!*" they kept saying, five-against-one on the rear deck of the Beach.

The passenger reached into his pocket. It was obvious what the Zairian police were after. All knew that they were underpaid, and also that they were among the elite who had jobs even if in name only.

All heads leaned forward to see—not so much the act of paying the extortion, as to see the *amount* it would take. In full view of the forty witnesses, the undocumented traveler took out the equivalent of thirty-five cents U.S. and handed it to the border police, who took it and went away.

We also saw women carrying contraband textiles, first from Brazzaville to Kinshasa, then again with the same items in the opposite direction, strapped to their backs to make them look like babies. Police let these peccadilloes go, knowing the women with textiles-as-babies couldn't have come up with cash for bribes or extortion.

Landing on the Brazzaville side after this half day in Kinshasa, I might have kissed the ground.

Months later, as Brazzaville police were learning from their clan brothers how to git up Westerners in the streets, they stopped me three times the same day, noting that my Mobylette might have some esoteric violations of local code in the exact configuration of the headlight.

"Your headlight seems incorrectly focused for night vision," they said.

When hit up for the third time the same day, I reached out with my two wrists and said, "If I am guilty of a crime, I demand that you handcuff me, take me to the police station and arrest me as a violator of local code. Do it now, please." They laughed and let me go.

The spirit of Kinshasa's "Heart of Darkness" perpetuated itself to August, 2018, when war criminal Jean Philippe Bemba tried to return to the country in advance of long-awaited elections there. He was stopped at the border. Of all the indecent players, all generally distasteful, Bemba was singled out on that particular day as somehow worse than the others, and denied entry into his native country. Maybe it was good that this criminal was blocked from adding more toxicity to his country during an election period. But relative to the others, he probably wasn't much worse.

Western chroniclers like to present obscurantist and deviant examples of their experiences in Central Africa, trying to impress the reader with derring-do and high-minded sniffling at injustices. In this, they are pale pretenders to the notoriety of the Stanleys and Burtons and Brazzas. This is not a meaningful contribution to understanding. The Beach, the police, the women carrying textile contraband, all figure into a picture of a broken system, and what then? In the 1980s, the Brazzaville side was marked by a greater humanity and humor than the Kinshasa side. Same languages, ethnic backgrounds, daily challenges testing the decency in individuals' actions and behavior.

Brazzaville at least had an ideology, and to its credit, one that nobody there ever believed.

Pietro Paolo Savorgnan di Brazzà

The more we learn about Brazzaville's namesake, the more interesting he becomes. Born of Italian nobility, Brazzà dreamt in his teenage years of joining the French navy as an officer. At a time which overlapped with the Garibaldi liberation efforts eventually leading to a state called "Italy," Brazzà was swept up in Romantic callings of human freedom and basic justice. Ample family support made it possible for him to devote himself to these goals.

Overlooked later in much of the world, Brazzà lived in France through the period of the Franco-Prussian War, the Dreyfus affair, the Berlin Conference carving up Africa for European colonization, and the peak period of exploration and colonization by British, Belgian, and French teams jockeying for position on the Continent. He took seriously the liberty-equality-fraternity principles of the French Revolution, and walked the walk toward universal application of those notions to Africa. Taking French citizenship in 1874, he renounced the modest seniority he had earned in the French navy prior to that time, in order to qualify for it.

The Congolese in Brazzaville remember him fondly to this day. He worked to suppress the slave trade—first in what is now Gabon, whose capital Libreville was named after "freedom" from slavery—and later on the Right Bank of the Congo River. During his explorations in Gabon, he was approached one night at his encampment by a slave trying to escape his owner. Brazzà purchased the man so as to free him. French policy encouraged the suppression of the slave trade, still vibrant on the coast of central Africa—though greedy commercial interests flagrantly broke the rules. Brazzà devoted the second half of his life to realizing the principles of French policy. He made enemies doing so, including the predatory Henry Morton Stanley. Stanley detested Brazzà, and did everything to undermine his efforts.

At a high-profile dinner in 1882 at the Paris Geographical Society, Brazzà was caught up in traffic, and Stanley seized the moment to vilify his rival as a hypocrite and incompetent. Stanley was enraged at Brazzà's effrontery in claiming the right bank of the Congo for French dominion. King Leopold's pimp, Stanley brought confrontation, murder and slavery to the areas he ravaged.

When he arrived late to the dinner, Brazzà responded simply, "I understand, *cher collègue*, that you have roughly attacked me in your speech. Before I learn what you actually said, let me shake your hand." He knew how to win an audience over.

Brazzà did everything he could to uphold often-betrayed French principles of equal treatment before the law. He offered himself to the French government to inspect, condemn, and correct the human rights abuses that occurred in central Africa after his explorations, at the hands of French commercial interests. What changed everything was the advent of the bicycle, and later the automobile, which created a sudden demand for rubber from the colonies. The executions, amputations and other punishments for Africans failing to meet their quota of harvested rubber from the trees in the Congo basin were covered up in the 1890s, but exposed in the 1900s. Brazzà's efforts to counter these abuses ran up against powerful commercial interests, but also their powerful allies in the French government.

Brazzà was a rock star in late nineteenth-century France, and drew enormous crowds during his rare sojourns in Paris. At his funeral in 1905, thousands of Parisians stood along the procession along the rue de Rivoli to show their respect. The crowds almost rivaled those of the immense Victor Hugo commemoration from twenty years earlier. The French mainly revered Brazzà, though later in his life he was maligned as a not-so-French import. Efforts to discredit him as a "foreigner" came at about the same time as the efforts to denounce Dreyfus as a not-so-French (Jewish) officer. Dreyfus, exonerated in 1906 after seven years of persecution for treason, still was castigated by nativists similarly to the way they had gone after Brazzà. Both were attacked by those who tried to frame them as outsiders.

In his three expeditions to Central Africa, Brazzà learned the customs and rituals of the communities he visited, and earned the friendship and loyalty of many. He listened carefully, followed local protocol to show respect, made sure his ideas and proposals were faithfully interpreted in local languages to avoid misunderstand-ings. He used diplomacy to win trust among his own colleagues and local populations. He had devoted subordinates—Alfred Marche, Noël Ballay, and Senegalese guide and interpreter Mala-mine Camara. Congolese local leader Makoko, sometimes thought to be "duped" by Brazzà's treaty of friendship under French sover-eignty, was in fact aware of the deal he signed with the French state in 1885, and saw the alliance as helpful to him in combating local rivals.

Brazzà became the governor-general of the area (the French Congo) 1886-97, until he was taken down by scheming business-men when he tried to downsize the revenue flowing to the French state from the colony. He was overtaken by events, embittered by the sadistic acts committed in his name in the Congo. Maybe na-ively, he had believed local and European interests could advance together in tandem.

Brazzà became a Freemason in 1888. He died September 14, 1905.

Buried in Algiers with his wife Thérèse de Chambrun, he was disinterred a hundred years later, his remains transferred October 3, 2005, to the opulent mausoleum in Brazzaville built just for the occasion. President Chirac of France attended the ceremony with President Sassou-Nguesso of Congo, and Ondimba of Gabon and three other African heads of state. Criticized as an extravagance the Congolese government could not afford, the mausoleum honored Brazzà's efforts to free African slaves in the last decades of the nine-teenth century.

Most African leaders who attended the building's inauguration were Freemasons, as Brazzà was. Coincidence? Make of that what you will.

Three

Civil War 1997-1999

Of Congo's traumas, the conflicts of 1997-1999 rank among the cruelest, most destructive, confusing, and pointless.

Though I wasn't in the area at that time, I believe any account of the country's recent history calls for a glance at this. I have stitched together transcripts of interviews on line, plus some oral histories I recorded in Brazzaville in 2018, and in Washington 2019.

The destruction and human suffering were caused not specifically by ethnic or ideological motives, nor even personal ambition, though the latter played its part. Opportunism and greed flowed from the top three factions down to the foot soldiers, who looted and taunted, seeing their booty as the just rewards of battles won. Sassou-Cobras; Lissouba-Cocoyes (aka Zulus); Kolélas-Ninjas. There were regional differences, with Sassou promoting the north, Lissouba the south, and Kolélas the southwest. Maybe something like what occurred in Sarajevo, Bosnia in the1990s. Ethnic groups lived in harmony with one another in the capital until the conflict broke out, with the city's neighborhoods becoming microcosms of the regional and ethnic divisions exacerbated by the war. Battle lines in the city reflected the demographic makeup of Poto-Poto, Makélélé, Mpila, Bacongo. These differences were entirely unknown to many expatriates until the hostilities broke on the night of 4-5 June, 1997. Troops loyal to President Lissouba surrounded ex-President Denis Sassou-Nguesso's compound in Mpila. Sassou's Cobra militia responded in force.

All factions were heavily armed, loyal to no one in particular, and frequently shifted sides to be with the likely ultimate winners. Of the three instigators, the only one left standing at the end was Denis Sassou-Nguesso. Sassou went on to be one of Africa's longest lasting rulers. As of this writing, Sassou has been in power well more than twice the time of, say, Vladimir Putin in Russia.

The parties pivoted unpredictably between savagery and courtesy. When American citizens were captured unwittingly, the captors dutifully called the U.S. Embassy and assured their safe return. Courageous African American diplomats at the Embassy were at increased risk, sometimes mistaken in the streets for local militia members, but ultimately they went unharmed. While shelling penetrated most areas of the city and put all at risk, Americans and their local employees were never targeted. (Some of the latter were killed in crossfire). Congolese belligerents generally saw the United States as unrelated to the problems. Less so, the French. Knowing this, the French had invested in a more robust local military protection.

Expatriates of many countries worked together and pooled resources for their common safety. No Congolese group benefitted from such assistance or safe haven. Fleeing the country was nearly impossible even from the beginning of the conflict, as ferry boats to the Kinshasa side of the river ceased operating.

For the transcripts on line (Phillips and Hooks) I gratefully acknowledge the Association for Diplomatic Studies and Training, Arlington, Virginia. I conducted other oral histories myself.

For brevity, I have condensed the content. For my own interviews, I have used paraphrase in addition.

Les Trois Glorieuses

On the three days of July 27-29, 1830, Charles X the Bourbon king of France was confronted, and convinced to abdicate, in a popular revolt intended to stem the political backsliding following the Revolution of 1789. The aims of social equity and rule of law, so loftily declared earlier, were mainly discarded in the decades after Napoleon's fall and exile. The so-called July Revolution of 1830 never achieved much, but did at least replace one monarch with another—Louis Philippe, Charles's cousin from the House of Orléans. Popular sovereignty replaced hereditary rule at least in theory, though Louis Philippe never quite caught the spirit of the new order, and was in turn overthrown in the so-called February Revolution of 1848. And so on, to the Commune of 1871 and beyond.

Nations are expected to come into existence through acts of courage, tempest, convulsion. Congo-Brazzaville lacked such a narrative in 1960 when the French simply declared it an independent country after granting autonomy to it in 1958. Congo needed a more heroic founding legend, and so keeps the memory of its own *"Trois Glorieuses"* during demonstrations in Brazzaville — not against the French, but those against Congo's first president, the Abbé Youlou — in August of 1963. The phrase evoked the 1830 movement in France, where the *"glorieuses"* referred to the three days in 1830, when street fights led to the end of the reign of Charles X.

The Brazzaville revolt not only was free of animosity toward the former colonizing country, it even officially thanked French President De Gaulle for judicious restraint in allowing the Brazzaville events to unfold without French intervention. *"Trois Glorieuses"* had other echoes, such as the three days of July 26-28, 1940, when Gaullists took command of French Equatorial Africa (AEF) preemptively during the early days of World War II, as the Vichy government was being formed.

The *"trois"* in Brazzaville, 1963, referred to days of conflict (August 13-15), but also to three martyrs taken away and shot during the uprising against the Abbé Youlou. Later a fourth was found dead, but for the sake of narrative, the phrase stuck as the moment of national liberation. The uprising among students and trade unionists transferred power to Alphonse Massamba-Débat and his MNR, National Revolutionary Movement. Youlou was a northerner, Massamba-Débat a southerner.

Though Massamba-Débat had good leftist credentials and openly supported the left-wing MPLA in Angola, and Lumumba in the former Belgian Congo, he lasted only five years. In 1968 a military coup transferred power back to the north, bringing in Marien Ngouabi, and taking the country further to the left while renaming the country "Peoples Republic of Congo." The PCT, Congolese Workers Party, replaced Massamba-Débat's MNR as the sole legal party.

Marien Ngouabi lived only thirty-nine years, December 31, 1938 - March 18, 1977. From humble background, he had set up a battalion of paratroopers in the Congo Republic as a junior military officer. Outspoken in his defiance of Massamba-Débat, in 1966 Ngouabi was demoted to soldier second class when he turned down a second posting to Pointe Noire on the coast. Two years later he was arrested for insurrection, but mobilized other Congolese military to work against the head of state. In different circumstances this could have been seen as treason, but after only two days in detention, Ngouabi was rescued by civil defense forces and promoted to head of the National Revolutionary Council July 31, 1968. Fate went his way two months later when Massamba-Débat was deposed in a military action resembling a coup. Ngouabi suddenly rose from his humble military commission to be head of state, with a trade unionist agenda.

The country now had a narrative to go by, but still lacked a national martyr until 1977. That year Marien Ngouabi sensed his popularity was slipping, and gathered his most loyal colleagues in secret, to propose the following: "kidnap" him and let the people imagine the worst, then arrange for him to reappear—again after *three days* to keep the theme consistent—at which point he would "rescue" the country from right-wing plots and rejoice at his return.

The problem was that one of the team doing the kidnap didn't understand—perhaps had not read the memo through to the end, and understood that his task was to kill Marien Ngouabi, and therefore did so. This was not in the letter or spirit of the scheme, and really spoiled the effort as well as ending the Marien Ngouabi period by putting him to death. (Whoops!)

The country went through further political spasms for another two years until northerner Sassou Nguesso took over in 1979, banning all political parties except his own Congolese Workers Party (PCT). With some interruptions, Sassou stayed until 2019 and beyond.

With Marien Ngouabi's death by "assassination," the country now had its own *trois glorieuses* from 1963; and in 1977, a national martyr as well. History-conscious, the Brazzaville Congolese had come to some peace with a colonial past which was more benign than that of the former Belgian Congo. And in addition, it had gained a heroic foundational legend.

March 18, the day of Ngouabi's assassination in 1977, is still commemorated as Marien Ngouabi Day.

"Better to lose the Congolese than the Congo"
Attributed to Jacques Chirac, Elysée Palace June, 1997

"Attributed," because it seems the comment was never recorded or transcribed. It may be urban legend, but it comes up repeatedly in individuals' accounts of what happened in Congo-Brazzaville during its civil war of 1997-99.

The French role in this nasty conflict was pretty clearly a matter of protecting its petroleum interests. Elected in 1992, President Pascal Lissouba had wanted to increase the share of profits going to the Congolese people from a paltry seventeen to a still modest 34 per cent. Not all that revolutionary, you would say. Actually, he wanted to go fifty/fifty, but dialed back his demands for a fair share of the money coming from petroleum exports drilled on Congolese soil. Lots of killing and displacement seemed the acceptable collateral damage to go with keeping the prices at gas pumps in France at pre-1997 levels.

By contrast, individual Congolese actors were complicated, with close alliances later murderously broken, and power grabs for stakes that seemed insignificant to outsiders, but were all the Congolese had to fight over. I remember reading about this war from my home in Pretoria at the time, and thinking, "Sweet Moses, even that harmless country has splintered and fallen on itself."

Getting from the presidency of Denis Sassou-Nguesso of 1979 to the one of today is anything but a straight line. Militias appear: Sassou's Cobras, Kolelas's Ninjas, Lissouba's Cocoyes. Sassou makes his peace with former enemy Lissouba in 1993 and joins him in a coalition government in 1995, only to prepare his own real return by force in 1997. Lissouba's Cocoye forces then challenge Sassou, and a destructive civil war breaks out. Ethnic tensions erupt in formerly peaceful Brazzaville, leaving many displaced and tens of thousands dead. Kolélas's Ninjas make a jab for power during the tumult, but are beaten back. Angola's military intervenes for Sassou and gets him back to power, taking up again from where he was 1979-92. The French approve. Americans backing Elf's rival, Occidental ("Oxy") fold at the gaming table.

In working on this chapter, I realized I had never really kept straight the militias, leaders, northerners, southerners, ideologies shifting kaleidoscopically. So I charted them out. It went something like this:

84		*Back to Brazzaville*

Dramatis Personnae

Denis Sassou-Nguesso, born 1943, president 1979-92 and 1997 to the present. Militia, Cobras. Party leader of the **PCT, the Congolese Workers Party**, founded in 1969 with a Marxist-Leninist line, though friendly to French, and French commercial interests. A Northerner.

Pascal Lissouba, born 1931, the first and possibly the only democratically elected president in Congo-Brazzaville's history, August 31, 1992 - October 24, 1997. A Southwesterner. Militia, Cocoye (aka Zulu) Party, **UPADES, the Panafricain Union for Social Democracy**. Prime Minister 1963-66 under President Massamba-Débat. Implicated in the 1977 assassination of President Marien Ngouabi and sentenced to hard labor, then exiled in France. Elected president in 1992, Lissouba swung the country to the right, supporting rightwing UNITA rebels in Angola, openly spurning the president of France for grabbing the Congo's resources. (UNITA, the National Union for the Total Independence of Angola, sought to overthrow the ruling Marxist Popular Movement for the Liberation of Angola, MPLA). Lissouba overthrown in 1997 by Sassou.

Bernard Kolélas, 1933-2009, Pool region. Foreign Minister under former president Massamba-Débat, later came in second in the elections of 1992, became mayor of Brazzaville. Militia, Ninjas; party, the **MCDDI, the Congolese Movement for Democracy and Integral Development**. History of political actions in 1963 resulting in exile to Kinshasa 1964, then attempted coups (1969, 1978) imprisoned four times, sentenced to death in absentia May 4, 2000, granted safe passage to his wife's funeral October 2005, amnestied by President Sassou November 23 of the same year, elected to National Assembly 2007.

Time Sketch, pre-independence to 2018

1958 Granted autonomy by de Gaulle within the French Customs Union.

1959 uprising from a French-trained customs official, who says,

"You trained me to combat corruption, so I am doing as you said." Some date Congo's restless recent history from this time.

August, 1960, independence. President (northerner) Abbé Fulbert Youlou, marked by corruption, lack of French assistance.

August 13-15, 1963. "Les Trois Glorieuses" uprising by students, labor unionists, and the military, overturned Youlou.

1963 Alphonse Massamba-Débat (southerner) takes power with the **MNR, National Revolutionary Movement.** Massamba-Débat germinated the future leftward tilt of the country, supporting Angola's Marxist MPLA and offering asylum to Patrice Lumumba in Congo-Kinshasa before the assassination of the latter.

1968 Military discontent with power concentrated in the south stages a coup, brings down Massamba-Débat, installs (northerner) Marien Ngouabi, taking the country further to the left and renaming the country "Peoples Republic of Congo." The **PCT, Congolese Workers Party**, replaces Massamba-Débat's MNR as the sole legal party.

March, 1977 Marien Ngouabi assassinated in a plot involving southerners wresting back power to their region. Briefly followed by (northerner) Joachim Yombi-Opango but "replaced" by (northerner) Colonel Denis Sassou-Nguesso, 1979.

1979 New Constitution under Sassou-Nguesso, outlining a Marxist-Leninist platform. Friendly, however, with France.

1980 Summit at Baule, France: President Mitterrand encourages all former African colonies to adopt multiparty systems.

1991 Under mounting international pressure, the PCT agrees to a National Conference, permitting competing parties. Naissance of MCDDI (Kolélas) and UPADES (Lissouba). Euphoria under PM André Bilongo (now with the World Bank). Sassou organizes elections, planning to win them.

1992 Elections. Lissouba wins with the support of the three most populous regions (south) in the country—Bwenza, Niari, Lekoumou. After Lissouba in order of votes come Kolélas (Pool), André Milongo (Lari in southwest), Sassou (north).

1992 Kolélas takes his Ninjas over in support to Sassou's Cobras, the latter trained as regular military under the previous Sassou period. Sassou goes home to Oyo in the north, to pout and plan his return to power. He broods for four years in the north, and builds up training and materiel to bolster his Cobra militia. Gains clandestine support from France and neighboring countries.

1993 Lissouba refuses to give a cabinet portfolio to Kolélas. (Four years later, Lissouba and Kolélas, both in exile, unite their Cocoye and Ninja forces against Sassou). Skirmishes between two southern groups—Kolélas's Lari and Bacongo vs. Lissouba's Bembe and Diata.

1994 France's Elf/Acquitaine oil conglomerate appeals to France's Chirac against Lissouba's effort to take 34 per cent of the oil revenues for Congolese public coffers. Lissouba further alarms the French by reaching out to American-owned Occidental Oil ("Oxy") for alternative arrangements. Elf/Acquitaine, traditionally the donors to balance payments in the Congolese governments and pay salaries of civil servants, punitively withholds all funds and leaves Lissouba exposed to national bankruptcy.

1997 Sassou received "like a king" in the northern town of Owando. ("The war's origin") Ninjas try to block his entry; his Cobra militia responds with live ammunition, killing some, including an officer in Lissouba's regular army.

June 5, 1997 Lissouba unwisely moves to have Sassou arrested, establishing *casus belli* for Sassou to reenter Brazzaville by force from his northern redoubt in Oyo. Sassou reaches out to Kolélas for assistance, and enters a de facto alliance with his former foe. The U.S. embassy, under crossfire and attacked by mortars and small arms, evacuates Americans to Kinshasa, and advises local staff to shelter in place. They do so, unable to leave the premises for three months.

1999 National Dialogue, with new constitution January 1, 2002.

2002 After relative peace, Sassou is reelected in March; conflict again breaks out in the Pool region. Many displaced in the south.

2003 relative peace returns.

2009 Elections boycotted by the opposition go easily to Sassou.

2012 Legislative elections July-August. Rumors of a ploy to allow Sassou to escape term limits. Sassou's PCT wins three out of five of the seats in the National Assembly.

2015 Term limits for the president removed at a National Forum.

2016 Though contested and under dubious circumstances, the presidential elections go to Sassou in the first round. March 20, he declares himself the winner.

Lissouba's fatal errors *(This merits a separate comment).*

He failed to establish a constitutional court. His foes used this to great effect.

He challenged Elf/Acquitaine, the Crown Jewels the France of the 1990s.

He opened dialogue with Elf's American competitor Occidental ("Oxy").

He insulted Jacques Chirac in Brazzaville.

He supported reactionary forces in Angola and elsewhere.

He fired fourteen generals from the army emboldened by its creator, Sassou.

He tried to arrest Sassou June 5, 1997. Bad move.

Any one of these *faux pas* would have done him in. Committing all of them made his downfall inevitable.

There is more, much more. The material above serves merely as context for the verbatim accounts in the chapters that follow.

Here are some "takeaways" from Congo's convoluted turn-of-the-century tensions:

Note from above, the sole consistent theme in establishing parties of conflict is *regions*: north, south, Pool. Beware charlatans who characterize these events as "ethnic" or "ideological." In demonstrable cases in Congo-Brazzaville's history, adversaries shared language and ethnic background. Unknowing journalists and ill-informed diplomats read identity falsely as the "cause" of the conflict.

Whence, then, the conflicts? Power grabs between and among manipulators able to alarm, excite and mobilize gullible citizens, motivated more by fear than hate.

How did the manipulators manage this? As little as one per cent of the population finds ways of forging harmony and loyalty with 2-3 per cent more, usually through propaganda or favors to outsiders like unemployed young men. The remaining 97% are merely observers and victims.

The superhuman talent of manipulators (see Genghis Khan, Richard II, Don Juan, Napoleon, twentieth-century dictators, Dick Cheney) exceeds in energy and imagination of the majority of any population. They think and act on a plane not even perceived by the many. Self-aggrandizement exceeds self-defense, as the machine gun exceeds the butter knife as weapon.

Alliances are based on expediency, not mutual interest or values.

All parties in conflicts fight because of their perception—real or imagined—as being victims. Bullies, we often note, are the first to feel fear. Their fear stirs an intensity of motivation we cannot fathom or effectively counter.

As the banners of loyalty go up in battle, we remember that banners (and "identity") are the consequence, not the causes of the battle. "They" hurt "us," so we rise up for retaliation and protection. Hence the cycle of violence continues for decades, centuries, until someone goes by the Golden Rule to halt the lethal logic.

Goodness and villainy commingle in every soul. Ambiguity is the platform for understanding.

Conflicts are managed, not "resolved." Exhaustion and extermination are the only sure paths to cauterize and relegate them to history.

Congo-Brazzaville is not unique in its patterns of conflict, but is a worthy case study.

Injustice is as strong a motivator as fear—possibly stronger.

And some words on history itself

Short of spooky life-after-death scenarios, history is the best instrument we have for rendering judgment. All people crave judgment, and want positive judgment of themselves. Not for nothing, judging and being judged are themes of popular entertainment.

"Narrative" is anyone else's version of events which differs from mine.

Humans need to tell stories, and hope someone listens to them. They are advised to listen to stories themselves, though often they don't.

Here below are some seven accounts, translated and redacted from interviews I recorded in French during the summer of 2018. I've omitted references to objective historic fact where they duplicate the time line above, and have stuck mainly with the personal accounts. I have scrambled the names, aware that anyone can be vulnerable at any time to persecution.

With gratitude and credit to the Association for Diplomatic Studies and Training and ADST's Stu Kennedy, who conducted the interviews with Ambassadors Phillips and Hooks, cited below. And for the Congolese willing to tell their stories to me, all of them sharing lasting injury. They knew their adversities of 1997-99 had never attracted much attention, nor are even known by most of the world today.

Ambassador James D. Phillips
Interviewed by Charles Stuart Kennedy May 5, 1998
Association for Diplomatic Studies and Training

The focus of this section is the full-scale conflict of 1997-99. Nevertheless, context comes in the precursor events of 1990-91, when internal alliances formed, dissolved, and external corporate pressure (Elf/Aquitaine) came with the full-throated support and connivance of the French government. In his open source interview with Charles Stuart Kennedy, James D. Phillips renders his version of the 1990-91 events in Brazzaville, from when he was ambassador there 1990-93. His account parallels, but does not exactly match, some of the versions I recorded in summer of 2018 with Congolese citizens caught in the crossfire. Below, Phillips's words, shortened for this book.

> The Congo had been a Soviet enclave. Brazzaville is right across the river from Kinshasa. If you think of Minneapolis and St. Paul, that is the relationship between Brazzaville and Kinshasa. It could be one city divided by a river. It was a listening post for the Soviets, a window on Angola, Zaire, and all of Central Africa. It was an island of Soviet influence in the middle of a very troubled sea. One of our main interests was simply to know what the Soviets were up to.
>
> When I got there, Sassou-Nguesso was President. He had been elected like other communist leaders in sham elections and had been in power for fifteen years. There was a huge Soviet, East German, North Korean and Chinese presence and just a smattering of Western embassies. On the economic side, oil had been discovered offshore near the Atlantic port city of Pointe Noire. Congo's offshore fields are part of a vast area of oil deposits stretching down the Atlantic coast from Nigeria to Angola. Some analysts believe depos-

its in that area are equal to those in the Arabian Gulf. The oil is readily accessible because of new deep-water drilling technology. It is attractive to oil companies because they can add to their proven reserves. They love to have known deposits they can draw on when the time is right. If the Soviets were the most influential power politically, the French were the most influential economically.

Elf, the French quasi-national oil company, developed the oil fields and had worked out a very cozy relationship with Congo's political leaders. If you want to see corruption at its worst, put together an international oil company and a communist dictatorship. There are absolutely no controls. No free press. No checks and balances. Elf was rather handsomely taking care of top Congolese officials and party leaders, probably not more than three hundred prominent families, and creaming off the rest for itself. American companies wanted to do business with the Congo even though it was a Marxist state, and they had made some inroads into what the French regarded as its special sphere of influence. Conoco, Chevron, Citizens Energy, Amoco and Apache all had a foothold in the Congo. They were mainly working in areas Elf had rejected. Amoco had some production and the others had drilling rights. Just a bit south in Angolan waters Chevron had huge offshore production. So, a major interest of the United States was to try to assure that American companies were treated fairly in a difficult environment marked by strong Soviet political influence and French economic ascendancy.

President Sassou-Nguesso was in his mid-forties. He had a daughter in her twenties who was engaged to marry the President of Gabon, Omar Bongo, a man in his sixties. It was a political marriage and a major event for both countries. The marriage was scheduled for a day or two after my arrival [1990] and the Chief of Protocol told me the President wanted me to attend the wedding and had arranged for me to present my letters of credentials immediately... Actually, I believe the Congolese were beginning to wake up to the fact that they weren't getting their fair share of the oil revenues and they wanted American oil companies to balance Elf's presence. So I was the object of a minor charm offensive.

Sassou-Nguesso was in power as the Marxist head of a one-party state. The embassy was organized as a listening post and an economic support post. We had almost no consular work. We had a cultural center which was a magnet for anti-U.S. protests. Relations were improving, however, because Chet Crocker, the Assistant Secretary for African Affairs, used Brazzaville as a base when he was trying to broker a peace agreement in Angola. Sassou-Nguesso had been helpful because it was in his interest to see the Angolan conflict resolved. That was the setting, and had business continued as usual, my life in Brazzaville would have been rather uneventful. But in September of 1990 a major labor dispute broke out that had unforeseen consequences.

The labor unions were normally part of the communist establishment, but because of changes in Eastern Europe and the decline of Marxist influence worldwide, the Congo's labor leaders were emboldened to challenge the regime. There was a strike that the government handled rather badly. Other dissidents began openly criticizing the regime and the security forces appeared unwilling or unable to crack down as they would have in the past. In fact, the Marxist regime was reeling. It could no longer convincingly justify its hold on power. A university professor told me it was as if people were waking up from a bad dream; they were asking themselves why they were on foot while party leaders were riding around in Mercedes. There was no lack of cause for popular resentment. For example, a beautiful, modern building in Brazzaville had been built with European assistance funds as part of the university. But instead of serving students, it was being used as headquarters for the youth wing of the party. It was a hangout for all the young Marxist thugs.

...Sassou-Nguesso tried to buy time by proposing new elections, but he was fast losing credibility. Opposition leaders came out of the woodwork and began insisting on a uniquely African institution called a "National Conference." The idea was to bring people together in a setting where everyone could have a say on the model of palavers held in African villages. The point of such a gathering was to establish procedures for adopting a new constitution and eventually electing a new government. Sassou-Nguesso fought the national conference idea tooth and nail, but it gained momentum and, in the end, he had no choice but to convene one. The National Conference met in the parliament building, displacing the communist legislators. It was a grass roots institution and was launched with high hopes.

The Congolese at this point were not relying much on outside help. What was occurring was a full-scale popular revolution, but a bloodless and disciplined one. I don't think the French immediately saw it as a Pandora's box in terms of their interests. As the National Conference progressed, however, it became clear that its participants harbored tremendous resentment against both the Soviet Union and France. Speaker after speaker demanded an accounting of the Congo's oil revenues, alleging they had been lost to Elf and government corruption. Speakers also expressed the strong belief that the ruling party could not have maintained its hold on power for so long without French complicity. But the aim of the conference was not so much to rehash the past as to build the future. Its main goal was to establish a transitional government that would organize democratic elections. The new situation brought dramatic changes for me. The new leaders expected support from the United States, particularly in preparing for elections. The difficulty was that Washington had a narrow focus in Africa, limited largely to South Africa and Angola, and had no budget for assisting emerging democracies like the Congo.

...What the Congo needed was assistance with transportation, communications, election materials and equipment—things that cost money. Neither official Washington nor the NGO community was prepared to provide that kind of assistance.

But let's go back to the late 1990-early 1991 period. The National Conference got off to a good start. The delegates elected a Catholic bishop as their presiding officer and set up committees to deal with legal, political, economic and social issues. They decided to choose an interim government to prepare for elections and manage the country until an elected government could take office. Two main candidates for the job of interim prime minister emerged. One was Pascal Lissouba, a well-educated biologist who had been jailed and then sent into exile by the communists. He had been living abroad for years, working for UNESCO. The second was Bernard Kolélas, a political activist who saw himself as the Nelson Mandela of the Congo. He had been tortured on several occasions by the government and would not hesitate to show you his scars. He had been a gadfly to the Marxist regime for twenty years. To his credit he saw that his election as interim prime minister might be too much for the Marxists to swallow. They still had the power to cause trouble, and Kolélas wanted to avoid a fight just then.

He planned to run for President eventually, and made the tactical decision to stand aside for a surrogate candidate named André Milango, an economist who had spent a number of years in Washington at the World Bank. Because Lissouba had lived in Paris while working at UNESCO and Milango had lived in Washington, the press and local political observers claimed that Lissouba was favored by France and Milango by the United States. Rumor soon had it that I was actively supporting Milango. The truth is that at that point I had never met either man. I think it is human nature to see politics as theater. It was inaccurate but made good theater to believe in a French candidate and a U.S. candidate. The National Conference was fairly evenly divided between Lissouba backers and Milango backers, but Milango was narrowly elected by the delegates. The National Conference started in December of 1990 and ran through July of 1991.

…During the transition period tensions with Elf flared up. The Milango government wanted to take a hard look at Elf's dealings with the former government, not least of all because when it took office the treasury was absolutely bare. There was literally no money in the till. But Elf stonewalled and the investigation got nowhere. The government then asked the World Bank to audit Elf's operations in the Congo, but again Elf refused to open its books. At about this time there was a big oil spill near Pointe Noire and Elf refused even to let the Minister of the Environment on its property to inspect the damage. Elf had been all-powerful in the Congo during the previous regime and was behaving as though nothing had changed. But the company was beginning to realize just how much reform could threaten its interests, and it lobbied the French government to put pressure on Milango to leave Elf alone. France became much cooler towards the new regime. Elf, for its part, apparently decided it would do whatever it took to maintain its dominance. It caused a great deal of trouble as the Congo's new institutions tried to take hold. Presidential, legislative and local elections were scheduled for the summer of 1991.

...The two first round winners in the presidential contest were Pascal Lissouba and Bernard Kolélas. Lissouba represented a coalition of related ethnic groups located in the center of the country, and Kolélas was the leader of the Bakongo people who lived in the heavily populated areas in and around Brazzaville. Lissouba won the run-off election with 64 percent of the vote, handily defeating Kolélas. He did so by forming an alliance with Sassou-Nguesso and several other political leaders who had been eliminated in the first round of voting. European and American election observers noted some irregularities but by and large judged it a free and fair election.

Kolélas, the persecuted, long-suffering opponent of the Marxist regime, could not believe that he could lose except through foul play. He protested loudly but got no international support for an investigation into alleged electoral fraud. There were rumors that France had given financial support to Lissouba's campaign and that the U.S. had done the same for Kolélas. I can't say what the French did, but I can assure you the United States contributed nothing to Kolélas. Because he needed a majority in the legislature, Lissouba was obliged to form a coalition government. He named a Prime Minister who began negotiations with the various parties.

The obvious partner was Sassou-Nguesso's old Marxist party, rebaptized a European style Socialist party, because it had thrown its support behind Lissouba in the second round of voting. Although it only represented eight percent of the vote, Sassou Nguesso's group demanded the key ministries of Interior, Defense, Finance and Energy. Some observers speculated that these demands were based on the simple arrogance of a party used to governing; others contended old regime activists needed powerful posts to stave off embarrassing investigations of their tenure in office. Whatever the reason for their demands, Lissouba and his Prime Minister were not about to give them that kind of power.

Nonetheless, Sassou-Nguesso and Kolélas began negotiating. About this time Kolélas asked to meet with me privately. I agreed and we met one evening at the DCM's residence...After some embarrassment, Kolélas told me he was about to form an alliance with Sassou-Nguesso. He explained that he still considered Sassou-Nguesso the devil incarnate, but that politics makes strange bedfellows. He claimed to believe Lissouba was potentially a worse dictator than Sassou Nguesso and that a political marriage of convenience was the only way he could be stopped. The idea was to form a bloc in the National Assembly which would vote to reject Lissouba's choice for Prime Minister. This would bring down the government because the constitution provided that the President had to select a Prime Minister from the ranks of the majority in the Assembly. If his nominee was rejected, Lissouba would have to turn to the Kolelas/Sassou-Nguesso newly minted majority for a Prime Minister, and by extension for his entire government.

...The Kolélas/Sassou-Nguesso alliance forced the new regime to confront the issue within weeks of its inception. I told Kolélas that I thought it was a terrible idea. Not only would he lose credibility by joining Sassou-Nguesso, he also risked throwing the country into chaos. I pointed out that the new institutions were in the infant stage, that no supreme court existed to sort out constitutional questions, and that average Congolese citizens had no experience with democracy, let alone with a democracy that posed complex constitutional issues only several weeks after a bitterly contested election. I argued he would be better off to accept the role of leader of the "loyal opposition." He would then be in a strong position to run again in the next elections.

Kolélas listened politely, but it was apparent he had made up his mind. Within the week the scenario played out as Kolélas said it would, but only partially. The new Assembly majority rejected Lissouba's prime minister, but instead of turning to Kolélas and Sassou-Nguesso in naming another one, Lissouba dissolved parliament and called for new legislative elections. The stakes were high. Sassou-Nguesso and Kolélas were trying to marginalize Lissouba by shifting power from the Presidency to the National Assembly. They were trying to win by constitutional maneuvering what they failed to win in the elections. Both sides dug in their heels; both honestly believed they were in the right. When it became evident that Lissouba was serious about dissolving parliament, Kolélas supporters staged a protest march in downtown Brazzaville. This is when the first blood was shed.

Lissouba's security forces confronted the marchers and shots were fired. About a dozen protesters were killed. This effectively polarized the country and created a situation marked by acrimonious charges and counter-charges. Both sides thought the constitution justified their position. A hostile standoff was created that lasted a long time. Lissouba called for new elections, but the opposition parties declared they would boycott them.

I met with both sides to try to get them to work out some kind of compromise, and eventually they did agree to a date and procedures for new elections. But this time it was the Lissouba administration that was in charge of organizing the elections, not a neutral transition government or a national conference. So the opposition was suspicious of every aspect of the preparations... Although European and American monitors had declared the second elections free and fair, suspicion and animosity now ran too deep for either side to back down. Political leaders began demonizing each other, political parties began recruiting and arming militias, and the country was on the brink of civil war. All sense of tolerance and national unity had been lost in the several months since the end of the National Conference. I don't know how many people were killed in the ensuing fighting, but I would guess that it was in the tens of thousands.

...The fighting was largely tribe against tribe. Political problems were becoming intractable and economic events were also proving to be divisive.

When Lissouba took office, he inherited an administration that was dead broke. He couldn't provide even rudimentary services. Civil servants hadn't been paid for nine months and there was no new money coming in to pay them. Elf informed Lissouba that the previous government had in effect mortgaged the Congo's royalty oil far into the future. Lissouba went to France hat in hand asking for financial support, and he did get a little from the French Government and from Elf, but he was infuriated by Elf's refusal to open its books. Elf was telling him basically to be a good boy and he would be taken care of. Lissouba refused to play along, and insisted that the Congo have at least treatment from Elf equivalent to that given to other Francophone countries such as Gabon. Elf at the time was operating like a state within a state, and the company turned on Lissouba when he became too insistent. Lissouba's relations soured not only with Elf but with France.

Politicians and journalists [in France] were either in the game or didn't care. Neither the Socialists nor the Gaullists wanted to upset Elf's apple cart. France saw its former African colonies as a special cultural and linguistic sphere of influence, and were paranoid about encroachments, real or imagined, by other countries, especially the United States. The French government was protective of Elf and began to see Lissouba as a threat to its political and economic interests not only in the Congo, but throughout Africa.

…Lissouba's early efforts to woo France failed, and by the fall of 1991 he was distinctly out of favor. France was disenchanted with the Congo's somewhat messy democratic movement, and Elf didn't hide the fact that it would have preferred to have Sassou-Nguesso back in power. But at first Elf 's tactic was simply to stonewall Lissouba whenever he requested a more open and beneficial relationship. Later Elf played hard ball. The trouble started when Occidental came in with a very high-powered team to try to win an offshore drilling concession. But the more Oxy looked at the Congo, the more it saw a unique opportunity. Meanwhile the Lissouba government was desperate for money.

Oxy [Occidental], however, had no qualms about helping Lissouba, and began negotiating for the outright purchase of the royalty oil. Both sides recognized the huge risk involved because of increasing political instability, so the price was advantageous for Oxy. But the deal was also advantageous for Lissouba because of the timing. He needed to pay the civil servants and show some financial benefit for the country to win the legislative elections and maintain his hold on power, and the Oxy deal was all that was available in the short run.

The result was that Lissouba agreed to sell Oxy the royalty oil plus drilling rights in two major offshore blocks for 150 million dollars. I was kept informed as negotiations went along, but I couldn't become directly involved as Ambassador because that would have been showing special favor to one U.S. company. Chevron and Amoco, for example, might have asked why I didn't do the same for them. But I was as supportive as I could be. Dave Martin, who was the president of Occidental Petroleum, called me one evening to say that agreement had been reached and that Oxy planned to transfer $150 million to the Congo.

I asked when, and he said, "Tonight." I suggested wiring the funds to the local branch of a Belgian bank. I knew the French would have fits when they found out about the deal and that money sent through the main bank in Brazzaville, which was French, might get conveniently "delayed."

...The next morning the astonished manager of the Belgian bank called me to ask if I could explain why he suddenly had 150 million dollars he didn't have yesterday. I told him it was for the treasury of the Congo, so he wouldn't have it for long.

When the French found out about the deal, there was a major hue and cry. Local French businessmen led by Elf accused the United States of trying to replace France in the Congo and perhaps in all of West Africa. This was absurd. All we wanted was a fair shake for American firms trying to do business in the Congo. We even advised U.S. companies that they had a better chance of succeeding if they took on a French partner. Elf knew this, but was terrified that opening the market to American firms would force it to open its books for public inspection.

Elf did not want to explain publicly why the Congo got

only thirteen percent of the oil produced on its territory while Gabon and other African countries got the normal 51 percent. Elf was in fact in the process of covering up a major scandal which eventually resulted in its CEO being fired and jailed, but at the time we are discussing, it was still all powerful. It had its own intelligence service and allegedly supplied money and arms to African allies when it suited its interests. It began actively opposing Lissouba and supporting Sassou-Nguesso. All of this occurred ten days before the elections. Lissouba used the money to pay the civil servants some six or seven months in salary arrears, which was wildly popular, and his party went on to win a majority of seats in the election.

Now the French were sure America had bought Lissouba and the elections. They did all they could to undermine the new Oxy/Congo relationship. Elf told Lissouba that if he would cancel the Oxy contract it would give him $150 million plus for the same deal, but Lissouba refused. He was pleased to have an American presence to balance Elf's power, and went so far as to request that Oxy provide him with a team of advisors to help him put the Congo's oil production on a more solid footing. In my view this was a terrible idea because I thought it would create unnecessary headaches and, in the end, would prove impractical.

Oxy thought Lissouba was asking for technical advisors and agreed. But the French thought he was trying to use Oxy for the much larger purpose of exposing Elf's corrupt practices. The French loved conspiracy theories and saw the whole thing as a design to exclude Elf from the very lucrative oil fields in neighboring Angola. Elf went ballistic, and the French government was almost equally upset. France saw Lissouba as nearly a traitor and began to behave accordingly.

My relations with Lissouba improved significantly, but unfortunately, I lost the trust of Sassou and even Kolélas because they thought the Embassy was implicitly involved in the Oxy deal and therefore in Lissouba's election victory. It took me some time to regain Kolélas's trust, and I never did reestablish particularly good relations with Sassou.

The final chapter in my Congo story is decidedly unhappy. Lissouba's coalition won the elections, but the results were violently contested by the opposition parties. There was no Congolese institution capable of resolving the dispute, and neither side would accept a compromise that excluded it from power. The country slid into a prolonged period of low-grade civil war. By low-grade I mean that there were never two fully equipped armies engaged in conventional warfare; rather, there were a series of guerrilla skirmishes fought by ragtag militias.

Of course Lissouba was able to rely on the Congolese army to some extent, but not entirely. He couldn't count on army elements from the northern provinces where Sassou's ethnic group held sway. There were strong indications that Elf supplied the opposition forces with money and arms, although I don't have concrete evidence of this. In any case, thousands of Congolese lives were lost. The violence was concentrated in the Brazzaville area and I had to evacuate non-essential Embassy personnel. The evacuations were complicated by the fact that Kinshasa experienced severe civil unrest at the same time. So we had evacuees coming across the river to Brazzaville, just as we were contemplating sending evacuees across to Kinshasa. In the end, both groups left from Brazzaville's airport which miraculously stayed open through all of the turbulence. Eventually both sides suffered enough casualties to become war-weary.

...That decision did not alter the majority in the National Assembly, and it confirmed Lissouba's hold on power, but the opposition was exhausted and accepted it. When I left in September 1993 a sort of uneasy peace had been established. The Embassy evacuees were able to return. Lissouba made Kolélas the mayor of Brazzaville and another opposition leader named [Jean-Marc] Thystère-Tchicaya the mayor of Pointe Noire. This helped the process of reconciliation, but did not go far enough. Lissouba feared and hated Sassou-Nguesso and refused to give him any sort of face-saving position. So that was the situation when I left the Congo.

As an epilog I can tell you that Sassou-Nguesso eventually mounted a bloody coup d'état with the help of French arms and Angolan soldiers. Our Embassy and residence were destroyed in the fighting. Sassou-Nguesso is once again President of the Congo. Lissouba is in exile in London. Oxy sold its interests in the Congo back to the government

... This is not to say that Washington was not supportive of Oxy and other American oil companies that tried to gain a foothold in the Congo. But there is support and there is support, and we were never prepared to go as far as the French in using political and diplomatic means to secure economic ends, at least not in France's African backyard. Oxy left the Congo voluntarily in 1995. Other American oil companies came in, but mainly as partners with French firms. When I left, Elf was still unreconstructed for the most part. It had renegotiated some contracts to give the country a better deal, but it was still profiting immensely from its Congo holdings. Since that time Elf has been entirely reorganized and privatized, and I understand it no longer operates as a state within a state....

Ambassador Aubrey Hooks
Interviewed by Charles Stuart Kennedy, September 5, 2009
Association for Diplomatic Studies and Training.

American Ambassador Hooks had a situation on his hands. After arriving in 1996, he sized up the country as well as he could, but no one could foresee what was to go down June 5, 1997. The Hooks account of events recounts blow-by-blow a conflict that was perilous for all, and certainly for United States diplomats caught in the crossfire. Vying local "leaders" abandoned alliances previously formed, and went all in for total control. This left Congolese citizens exposed to cruelties, official indifference to their plight, and subject to new traumas. Lissouba, Sassou-Nguesso, Kolélas silent in the background—had delusions of grandeur and put their own egos above the wellbeing of their citizens.

The Hooks account shows the characters in a tawdry Shakespearean drama sans elocution or elegance. Deputy Chief of Mission Vicente Valle took the risk of rescuing Americans caught at a checkpoint standoff. Valle later managed what was left of the embassy after its evacuation in summer of 1997.

The U.S. Embassy account gives one aspect of the conflict. Subsequent texts below, from Congolese witnesses, show the effect on the lives of those who lacked the option of evacuation.

Here is Hooks's account, edited for brevity, from his open source interview with Charles Stuart Kennedy in 2009, at the Association for Diplomatic Studies and Training:

> ...During my first year in Brazzaville, the country was moving toward elections to take place in July of 1997...The first elections in [1992] had gone reasonably well.
>
> Lissouba was really out of touch with reality. He was a chief in the old traditional style...I think Lissouba was afraid he would have difficulty winning the elections...although frankly, my own assessment was that he could have won them very easily...To be fair about it, Sassou was also preparing to disrupt the elections. Lissouba moved against Sassou very clumsily and things really went awry...The military was still loyal to Sassou. The military were mostly from the north of the country, and as soon as President Lissouba moved against Sassou, the military abandoned their posts, taking their weapons with them.
>
> ...During the conflict, the city was divided in half. President Lissouba's attack on Sassou's compound occurred on a Wednesday night, and on Thursday morning I got a phone call about 5:00 o'clock in the morning from one of Sassou's close confidants who later became minister of defense. He told me that Lissouba's tanks had surrounded Sassou's house. Lissouba was going to kill Sassou. He asked me to call Lissouba and get him to move the tanks back and stop the attack before it got out of hand.
>
> ...It was clear that President Lissouba had ordered this action. I knew we had a problem. I called the French ambassador to talk to him because the French were very clued in on things, but he was also surprised and was scrambling to gather facts as best he could. The situation immediately started degenerating....
>
> I went to see president Lissouba. His position was that Sassou intended to launch a coup d'état. Sassou had smuggled arms in preparation for the coup. Lissouba said he just could not tolerate this, the law is the law and he as presi-

dent had to [enforce] the law. I tried to tell him at the time, "Mister President, this is…getting out of hand. It is tearing this country apart. You are going into elections. You will probably win the elections."

He called it a police action. I said to him, "Even if you are able to overcome this action which is already getting out of hand, it is going to be difficult to repair the social fabric that has been torn apart." President Lissouba was really quite unrealistic in his outlook on the world. The situation on the ground was deteriorating rapidly.

…The embassy was located some 200-300 yards from the ministry of defense and we saw troops starting to head down to the shopping centers to loot. I called the president to tell him that his troops had started to loot. He said. "They are not my troops. These are just criminals."

I said, "Mr. President, they are your troops from the ministry of defense which I can look at. I can see the wheelbarrows and other things going from the stores back to the Ministry of Defense. I am an eyewitness to that."

"Oh," he said. "I will put a stop to that."

…We brought anyone to the Embassy who felt vulnerable, whose streets were being looted. The French were busy doing the same thing for French citizens. They had a far larger community than we did.

…I received a phone call from a frantic admiral in EU-COM [the U.S. military command responsible for Europe and Africa at the time] who said, "You've got to get out. The French are leaving." I said, "That's not right. I just spoke to the French ambassador this morning and they are bringing more troops." He said, "No, Paris just told us they are pulling their troops out of there."

I said, "This is news to me."

…When you've got difficult ties in Kinshasa or Brazzaville and lots of undisciplined troops along the river, anyone trying to cross the river is very vulnerable…At my request, EUCOM sent a team of twelve people with special skills who could help us coordinate with the French.

…[The French] decided to draw the line, and they were going to withdraw their troops, all of them. Basically, they decided they would not play the gendarme in the Congo,

and that the parties would have to work it out among themselves. I was in a predicament because EUCOM said, "We
want our guys out of there right now." I told them that I
was not leaving yet. We still had one Peace Corps volunteer
unaccounted for, a young woman who had left her village
on Wednesday to come to Brazzaville for a medical appointment. She had just disappeared along the way...I told EU-
COM that they could pull their team back but I would not
leave until Wednesday.

...We evacuated our guys from Brazzaville to Kinshasa
because I thought we could continue to function as an embassy from the Kinshasa side for a period of time.

...I was negotiating with the two parties to the conflict. I
went to see President Lissouba almost on a daily basis... Ini-
tially, we could go anywhere in the city with the flag flying
and get past roadblocks because neither side had a problem
with the United States...That began to change as the week
evolved. The soldiers began to get drunk from looted alco-
hol. They were poorly trained, poorly armed, undisciplined
and terrified. Obviously, no one was taking care of them.
Few if any meals were delivered to them. They had to fend
for themselves.

...Sassou and his troops tried an all-out attack to take
over the ministry of defense, located within sight of the
American Embassy, and the Presidency, on the other side
of the ministry of defense. We were right in the middle of
concentrated exchanges of firing. We had bullets pinging off
the walls and windows shattered.

...[We sent in two embassy cars to pick up American missionaries.] When the two cars arrived at the street
in question, they discovered that Sassou's guys had just
moved out and already controlled the area ... the defense
attaché decided the situation was too dangerous, and he
thought the rebels were going to kill the soldiers in his car.
I think he had a discussion with the rebels and just drove
away. They fired into the car trying to stop it. ...The car was
riddled with bullets at that point and the motor died. From
my window, I could see the defense attaché running toward
the embassy and I knew we had a problem.

...A local soldier took their radio and called me. He wouldn't let me talk to the American consul or the gunny, and I knew that was not a good sign. He said, "You've got fifteen minutes. You come and get them, you can have them..."

I had a tough decision to make, and I had little time to ponder the issue. I had to try to recover them by sending more of my people down there. Was this a trap or would they release them? ...It was probably the most difficult decision I had to make in my life. I thought if I don't make an effort to recover them, Washington is not going to appreciate that, and if I do make an effort to recover them and two more people are taken hostage, people in Washington are going to say, "How could you be so stupid?"

...I asked for volunteers. Another vice consul and the DCM [Deputy Chief of Mission Vicente Valle] volunteered to go. They were able to recover the gunny and the vice consul and that immediate crisis was over ... We could tell immediately that Sassou's troops were launching another attack on the ministry of defense.

...Sassou encouraged any and everybody to fight against President Lissouba. After the fighting was over and he took power, he no longer needed all those people; in fact, he didn't want them armed anymore. He wanted to control the situation...But what happens when the war is over? Sassou basically told the unemployed youth to give up their weapons and go back home. Well what's he got back home to go to? Unemployed, being a nobody? He doesn't like that... I suspect there were a few hundred that Sassou eliminated, and they tried to set themselves up as a power base and to control certain neighborhoods. There was ongoing violence in the city for a number of months.

...They looted my house as well, but only at the end. It was Sassou's troops that did it. A lesson to be learned is to leave every safe open, because the safes that were opened and had nothing in them, the looters didn't bother.

...My staff was drawn down quickly. Ultimately only the DCM and an admin person were left...When the war ended with Lissouba's flight out of Brazzaville, the Department asked that I return to Kinshasa. The Angolans helped to bring Sassou to power. The Angolan involvement had a lot to do with what was happening in Kinshasa because Mobuto had been supportive of [Angolan right-wing rebel] Savimbi, and Lissouba was vocally supportive of Mobutu. The French also decided that Lissouba was just crazy and unreliable, and it was time for him to go. Once the French and Angolans got involved, Lissouba's troops folded and Lissouba fled....

Vicente Valle
Interviewed by the author March 15, 2019
Washington, DC

Vicente Valle—"Vince" to most Americans—was deputy chief of mission in Brazzaville when the 1997 conflict broke out. Working closely with Ambassador Aubrey Hooks, he assisted in evacuating American citizens from the war zone. One of the last to depart himself, he managed the embassy remotely from Kinshasa, mainly by telephone. He returned to Brazzaville later during the conflict, and also in 2003 from Washington, when there still was not a U.S. Embassy in Brazzaville.

He made painful decisions, helping as many as he could. Though probably not targeted, two local employees were killed during the firefights in the capital. Looting and fractious conflict left the city in ruins, with the U.S. Embassy almost entirely destroyed, and most Americans' property trashed or stolen. The pace of the drawdown went by two criteria: (1) could the American Embassy assist in any way to mitigate the fighting? and (2) could the embassy team be sure that all American citizens were safe or evacuated? Only after the country team saw that the first objective was never going to work, and the second was achieved, was the withdrawal completed.

I spoke to Valle in his State Department office March 15, 2019.

Q: Your previous assignments?
VV: Abu Dhabi, Mozambique, Sumatra, Central America economics desk officer, econ section Paris, Caracas, then Deputy Chief of Mission Brazzaville starting summer, 1996.
[Valle served as executive director of the Association for

Diplomatic Studies and Training 2009-10, then later at the State Department's Office of Religious Freedom.]

Q: Why did the elections of 1996 go off track?

VV: The south had a larger population, the north sought to wrest control of the country away from southerner, President Pascal Lissouba. The north would likely not have won the election by votes, and other factors came into play. There was little sign of the impending troubles. Even just three days before the onset, I discussed the situation with a political scientist and he, also, saw nothing coming.

Q. Tell us about the management style of Ambassador Hooks, and the general morale at Post.

VV. Ambassador Hooks was hands-on, mindful of his employees and their needs, and open to suggestions and comments. The morale was quite good. There was golf, shopping at Score [the French supermarket in Brazzaville] and a generally good living situation.

Q. Was Sassou plotting his return even before the failed elections?

VV. Can't say for sure. But he knew the north would not come up with the votes to put him in to replace Pascal Lissouba.

Q. Your impressions of Lissouba, and did you meet him?

VV. I did. Not a born politician, I would say. He was more of an academician. He now lives in Paris. We believe he, also, was unaware of what was in store in summer of 1997.

Q. How did the day proceed?

VV. I was awakened by a call by the ambassador early in the morning. He told me Lissouba's troops had surrounded Sassou's compound in Brazzaville. It was clear trouble was on the way.

Maybe Lissouba had some inkling of a coming conflict, and wanted to preempt it. He misjudged. He likely didn't know that Sassou was so well prepared militarily for this action.

All factions had militias.

It wasn't easy keeping close track of events. For the first part of the morning things were just strange. The local employees at the embassy were anxious, but like everyone, were unable to predict what was to happen.

Q. The staff at the embassy?

VV. About ten-fifteen Americans, perhaps thirty-five to forty FSNs [Foreign Service Nationals, local employees]. Add to that the local guard force, which was contracted out by the embassy.

Things got much more complicated in the afternoon as checkpoints went up all over the city. Different factions set up barriers separately, leaving the situation very tense.

Kolélas's area, Bacongo, was largely peaceful. President Lissouba had "his" part of the city, and Sassou "his" own in Poto-Poto.

Looking back, I believe the fight was over power in general, and scarce resources in particular.

Q. What were people's motives in choosing sides?

VV. The young people in the militias turned quickly to looting; they wanted resources, food, domestic products before someone else stole them. Militia were involved, but so were others.

Q. How quickly did the embassy decide to draw down its American staff?

VV. Ambassador Hooks moved gradually but also quickly, in ordering the first part of the drawdown, so as to maintain control of the situation. After close communication with Washington, Ambassador Hooks directed a *partial* drawdown of staff quickly, so as to keep an active hand in the decision making. Washington followed Hooks's suggestions, understanding he was closer to the situation than they were. As we did our drawdown, Ambassador Hooks made sure to keep the minimum number of staff in place to run the embassy.

The situation became dangerous quickly. At first, our diplomatic license plates got through the roadblocks, respected by all factions. But later it became more risky. The city was paralyzed, and private American citizens needed to leave the country. Most of our efforts were to make sure all who wanted to leave were able to do so.

We chartered local airplanes including Air Kasai, consisting of a DC-3 and some other aircraft. Some were piloted by missionary services, some by private operators.

While this was happening, Ambassador Hooks was

very involved talking to all parties and seeking some sort of solution he might be able to assist with… We were looking at phased departure for staff.

Q. Lots of difficult decisions under the pressure of time.

VV. Yes. We were in the middle of the conflict, with heavy gunfire breaking out near the embassy. Very intense shooting. However, mainly we were not targeted.

Q. And on the second day?

VV. The second day, all American employees of the embassy moved into the chancellery and sheltered in place.

On the third day of the conflict, we requested special forces backup from EUCOM [the U.S. military command in Stuttgart which included Africa in its zone of responsibility.]

Ten ESAT [special forces] Americans arrived within twenty-four hours of our request, in a military transport plane from Stuttgart. Even as they landed, an intense firefight broke out in the city; there was nothing else to do than take the visitors with us to the safe haven of the embassy. The fighting was too intense for ten soldiers to be able to make much of a difference.

We lived in the chancellery for some time, along with FSNs who were able to make it into the building. Others stayed home. Because of security requirements, we could not allow the local employees into the controlled access part of the building, but encouraged them to stay wherever they were able. As shelling intensified and all took shelter under their desks, we had no way to know if they were alive or dead. Terrified, for sure.

The French ambassador meanwhile took an incoming missile in his office at the French Embassy. Luckily, he had stepped out the office to answer a call of nature down the hallway. But for that, he would have been killed.

Sunday of that week, on the third day of the conflict, two Americans were detained at checkpoints in the city. We were working to get Peace Corps volunteers into the embassy and out of the country. There were about twenty in the country.

The evacuation was conducted in phases, with most of it complete by the twelfth day of the conflict. We were not able to take local employees in the evacuation, but kept in close contact with them. Toward the end of our activities in country, we went down to the skeleton staff—the defense attaché, the admin officer, the ambassador, a communicator, and myself as DCM [deputy chief of mission]. The regional security officer was out of the country at the time, and the ambassador decided not to let him return. We also had a very brave consular officer, the gunny sergeant commanding the Marine detachment, and an acting defense attaché who filled in for the DATT [defense attaché].

Some Americans were caught in the crossfire. The acting DATT and consular officer bravely went out to the checkpoints to assist. As African Americans, the two were mistaken at times for Congolese, and possible members of rival factions. Once the local militias found out who they really were, they did everything to assure their safety.

So, two armored embassy cars were stopped at a checkpoint, facing Cobra militia. The Cobras fired on the first vehicle, cracking but not penetrating the heavy windows of the acting DATT's car. If the windshield had broken off, the driver and passenger would have been killed. Making it out barely, the acting DATT gunned the engine and managed to get through. However, now that he was beyond a checkpoint, the second car with the gunny sergeant and consular officer were stuck and captured at the check point. Ava Rodgers, the young consular officer, deserves special mention for her courage. So does William Rowland, our econ officer, who came with me when we went to retrieve Ava and the gunny from the Cobras.

RPGs [rocket-propelled grenades] were fired at the second car, but the armored windows held firm. When the Cobra militia figured out who the passengers were, they grabbed the Americans' embassy walkie-talkies and radioed us at the embassy.

"We have your people here, come and get them. Sorry, no harm meant," they said.

This was an offer we were glad to get. We couldn't exactly ignore it, even with the fire fights at an intense level in the streets.

When I arrived at the scene, the Cobra militia soldiers

were very polite and friendly. We were even inclined to converse with them. "Maybe it's time you left," they said. They knew they were planning an offensive at that time, and didn't want us to be in the middle of it.

Q. So, you were sheltering in place at the embassy and evacuating in phases. What about the FSNs [local employees]?

VV. We were very concerned about them, but the consensus was that we had to leave the city. On the twelfth day of the fighting, those of us still in Brazzaville took Air Kasai to Kinshasa. From the other side of the river we kept in close touch with the FSNs who had been able to make it to the embassy. We sent encouragement, requested that they protect the property as best they could. We kept them on the payroll by the way, and continued paying them by messenger from the Kinshasa side of the River.

The ambassador departed for Washington as we (myself and the admin officer the three others) made it to Kinshasa to "run" the embassy remotely. It was frustrating to manage things from that distance, not to say very difficult. To the U.S. Embassy in Kinshasa we were something of a burden. I stayed there for six months.

One FSN was detained and asked us for help. I called President Lissouba's chief of staff. I told her this was not tolerable, to detain an employee of the U.S. Embassy. She was savvy, and basically cooperative. We talked about this back and forth a bit. Eventually we managed to get our local employee released.

Meanwhile our employees trapped in the city had to go somewhere for food. One of the few options was a market in the Kolélas part of the city. It wasn't easy for them to get to market, so I called Kolélas, who was mayor of the city at that time. I got to talk to him directly. This was the sort of thing we were able to do remotely.

Finally, toward the end of the six months, only the admin officer and myself remained in the area. Ambassador Hooks had since been sent temporarily to be chargé d'affaires in Central African Republic, and also seconded at our mission to the UN in New York. He hoped he might be able to return to Brazzaville and pull things together, but it never happened.

After those six months it was time for me to leave. I'd had enough. Aside from the transient nature of daily living, there was also the frustration of trying to do anything meaningful in Brazzaville remotely by phone, plus the cold shoulder we were getting from some of our counterparts in Kinshasa.

By September of 1997, Angolan troops came in on the side of Sassou, and that pretty much settled the 96-97 phase of the conflict. There was another outbreak in 98-99.

Q. Did the French arrange the Angolan intervention?

VV. Possibly. I don't know for sure.

Q. Did you ever manage to make it back to Brazzaville?

VV. I did, in October of 1997. I went with the DATT [defense attaché] and RSO [regional security officer]. By then, the ferry across the river was back in operation.

We went to view the damage at the embassy. It was completely destroyed, then later burned. Nothing left. My own residence was looted, my personal car (with only 1000 miles on it!) stolen. After the conflict subsided, the Sassou militia went in and looted everything in sight. Dead bodies were still in the streets. Fish were probably gorging on human flesh of the dead who'd been thrown into the river. It was a bloody mess.

We confronted a looter driving one of our cars. He said, "I won this fair and square as war booty. If you want it back, you'll have to pay." Ambassador Hooks did manage to get a few things restored after talking to Sassou on the phone.

One local employee kept in touch with us in Kinshasa and came to collect the salaries of the others. He dutifully handed out the money to his colleagues back in Brazzaville. I think they were grateful that we continued paying them, at least I hope so.

Another embassy employee had worked for Sassou's previous administration. When his own car was stolen by pro-Sassou militants, he asked us to intercede. I reminded him that it was his own former colleagues who had stolen it, and suggested he get back in contact with them for compensation. Unfortunately, there was nothing we could do to help, since he didn't have diplomatic status.

One of our embassy guards was badly wounded in a firefight during that six-month period. He was coming off duty, and was being driven home by our local guard supervisor when he was shot for no apparent reason. The supervisor changed course and drove toward the hospital, but to no avail. The supervisor told us on the phone, "I tried. But he died in my arms." It was so frustrating to get this call and have no way to help from across the river. The relatives of our deceased colleague were of the Kolélas group, and blamed us for his death. That was when the Kolélas militia started hassling our guards when they tried to go through Bacongo.

The ambassador's former driver, meanwhile, was killed by an errant shell falling on his house.

After these six months I was feeling tired and frustrated. There wasn't much I could do from across the River. Finally, Ambassador Hooks did return to Kinshasa full time. I didn't see much point in having both an ambassador and a DCM at an embassy in exile, when we had almost no staff there. So I left. The ambassador meanwhile managed to meet with Sassou, and after much effort, he got Sassou to give us some of our stolen cars back.

Q. Lessons learned?

VV. Determine first what your objectives are, what it is you want. Ours were to try to ease the conflict, and make sure Americans were safe. When we saw the first was hopeless and the second was achieved entirely, only then did we begin a final drawdown of the embassy. Also, keep the risk/benefit balance in mind at all times. There will always be risk; you can only guess the best you can if the gain is worth it.

Also, call for help when you need to. Our American special forces arrived from Stuttgart within twenty-four hours. The French, also, with much greater military force in country, were able to help us. They kindly escorted us to the airport when we left by Air Kasai. In fact, all expats cooperated, including the Chinese, and we were in regular contact with them.

Of the Congolese themselves

Above, three accounts from dedicated American diplomats who put heart and soul into the country. They cared and took risks for themselves, their colleagues, and for the Congo. They were not targeted in the conflict, and had the means to depart.

Not so the Congolese themselves. A fuller understanding requires their accounts as well—personal sagas which did not always get into embassy reporting or Western journalists' versions of events.

Follows, four of those I conducted during summer of 2018.

Pascal's Story
University Professor

> Sassou and his PCT [Congolese Workers Party] contested the election outcome of 1992. Diplomats say the people were ok with Sassou. Not so! His strategy was to go to MCDDI [Congolese Movement for Democracy and Integral Development], which had some deputies in the National Assembly, and try to form an alliance with them and Kolélas. Together with Kolélas, they were able to put down UPADES (Lissouba). Sassou said that the real majority was not UPADES [PanAfrican Union for Social Democracy], but PCT together with MCDDI. He got his grip on Kolélas and left no way out.
>
> Sassou's Cobras [militia] came and trained Kolélas's people in the Ninja [militia], turning them against Lissouba and in favor of him, Sassou. They attacked civilians, with Cobra weapons. Lissouba was helpless, since "his" army was really Sassou's, trained by Moscow and Cuba, and remained loyal to Sassou.
>
> So Lissouba called up the reserves. This was not a real war. They attacked civilians attending funerals. The PCT provided weapons to the Ninjas, who by themselves were weak—just smoke to the fire of the Cobras.
>
> I saw houses being burned down. I am from the Pool, living in Bacongo, from the Lari group. The former prime minister, Milongo, is from the same background. So we

were all seen as Lissouba people, and were afraid to go out.

The Ninjas came to my house, and I had to run away. They took my motorcycle and destroyed my library. I lost everything. We weren't in agreement with what was happening, so we were seen as "infiltrators."

I fled to Moungali toward the northern part of the city, away from the worse areas like Bacongo. The war ended the MCDDI, Lissouba's party, at the hands of Sassou allies. Even Blaise Kouloulou, one of his allies, said, "This must be wrong. We're killing one another." But he pitched in and helped Sassou. The true enemy was not the Ninja themselves, but Sassou, who armed the Ninja.

So Lissouba hung on from 1992 to 1996, but the economy was based only on oil, and got weaker. Elf and Total distrusted Lissouba, especially when he said he needed 37 per cent of the oil profits for the Congolese. Lissouba brought in Chevron—the spark, the last straw—and Elf stopped sending money to Lissouba in order to sabotage him. The national budget was wrecked.

Sassou "retreated" to Oyo and asked to leave the country. Lissouba granted him this, and Sassou went to France. Once there, he plotted his return with Chirac's help. He also went to many other countries to recruit help. Even Mandela received him in South Africa in 1994.

By that time, we knew at the university what was going on, what Sassou was planning. As Lissouba began preparing the elections of 1997, he failed to set up a constitutional court—one of his fatal mistakes. The PCT took this as a pretext to denounce him. Then, in January-February of 1997, Sassou again returned to Oyo. There he organized political rallies, talking about "a better life post Lissouba." Lissouba's interior ministry told him he wasn't authorized to do this sort of thing, so he began organizing his military.

We knew things were going to be bad for southerners. I even turned down a teaching post offered in the north, where I knew it wouldn't be good for me.

Sassou needed to provoke an incident to spark the war. So he went to Owando, heavily armed, to organize a popular rally. Ninjas and others tried to block their way, but he shot into the crowd, then retreated to Oyo to see what Lissouba's next move would be.

Lissouba tried to sign an agreement with the United States. The U.S. ambassador was still in Brazzaville at that time. The war, meanwhile, went in favor of the Cobra, Rwanda, and Angola. Chirac organized interventions on the part of *ten* countries.

Lissouba tried setting up a constitutional court in order to keep power at least until elections, but Chirac cut him off from doing so. The International Court of Justice should have prevented all this.

Then came "The Terror" as I call it, in 1997. We who stayed behind were terrorized by Cobras, who raped and pillaged. By the end of that year Lissouba managed to flee to France, since as a citizen of the prior colony of Congo-Brazzaville, he kept his French citizenship. Those born in AEF— Afrique Equatoriale Française—never had their citizenship revoked. Even though we became "independent" in 1960, we kept French citizenship.

The Cobras continued to terrorize us in 1997, assisted by the Angolans. How could we get this to stop?

In December of 1998 the gunfire got closer and closer. Soldiers came with staff to confiscate people's belongings. They even took the World Health Organization headquarters. [WHO Africa headquarters are in Brazzaville.] We needed to escape, but didn't know it yet. The radio might have warned us, but we didn't know what was happening. We heard that the Ninja were pillaging the World Health Organization headquarters.

At 10:00 a.m. one morning, the Ninja went to Bacongo, where they were greeted as liberators freeing the people from Cobra terror. Heavy weapons fire came, however. We all fled on foot, going to Ndombmo-Mayanga. It took ten days to walk the 200 kilometers. There we stayed for one year. Others went to Pointe Noire on the coast, on foot. In Ndombmo-Mayanga, at least we were near DRC, and had salt and sugar.

In April of 1998 I wanted to take the ferry across the river, but there were roundups at the ferry crossing. So I waited until September. By that time, DRC was gathering refugees, and UNHCR [UN High Commission on Refugees] left us at the Centre Sportif where we were relatively safe.

As the war progressed, the Cobra invaded the Pool area and ransacked it. Finally, we crossed the river on foot at a land bridge up north, and from there made our way to Kinshasa. UNHCR organized convoys for those in Kinshasa who wanted to go back to Brazzaville. So by September 1998 we were mainly in the clear, though we had lost everything we had.

December 18, 1998, at 11:00 a.m. the Ninjas entered Bacongo, where they were cheered by the people. That is, we *thought* they were Ninja coming to free us. But in fact, they were wearing clothes inside out, and entered with mental patients as the army bombarded Bacongo.

We fled to the Pool region, where the purported "Ninjas" in fact threatened us, then said, "We are not Ninja!" Scary!

So, who were these soldiers, in fact? We kept our heads down. In the villages we saw these faux "Ninjas" pick up southerners and then take them off to kill them.

What on earth is going on?

Where did the weapons come from?

Where did they get their frequencies for their satellite phones??

If the Pasteur Ntoumi, supposedly in opposition to Sassou, had really come to mess up Brazzaville, Sassou's men would have gotten him. But in fact, he was working, all mixed in, with Sassou. This past month [July, 2018] they freed Ntoumi from detention because they [the Sassou government of 2018] knew they would soon need him as a phony "opposition" figure to make the elections of 2021 seem legitimate. It's all a ploy to take in naïve Westerners.

This will keep Sassou in place in 2021. There is NO real opposition; they are all working together.

In the 2015 legislative elections they posed as "opposition" in the Pool, but this was also a ploy.

What we have is manipulation, not really ethnic conflict. The politics of it is hiding behind a supposed "ethnic" issue. It's not.

Our groups, tribes, are gullible because we have no real political parties—the candidates play this fiction to get power.

At the U.S. Embassy you give us scholarships, but that isn't enough. All embassies must realize that any so-called "ethnic" party in the Pool is a phony one. If we had real political parties, based on political platforms, we wouldn't have these problems. In fact, there's no real political identity in Congo. If you define a party as an ideology, then you easily transcend tribal origins. Take the Socialists in France, for example. They represent people from all regions of the country. We don't have anything like that here.

Dieudonnée's Story
Housewife

I am from the Pool region. My father was a pharmacist. I was eight when the war broke out in 1997. People took what they could, and fled. They made for the Pont du Djoué and waited there to see what would happen, before fleeing to villages where they had relatives and friends.

With the economy collapsing since 1992-93, members of families took turns eating—the brother one day, the sister, the next. Students had to drop out of school. Lissouba lacked funds even to hold local elections, so in 1993 they weren't held. The masses turned against Lissouba, held him accountable for the economic debacle—Sassou at least had been able to pay his bills!

We never really found out why Lissouba tried to have Sassou arrested June 5, 1997. When that happened, militias and the army were all at war against one another. After we made it as far as the Pont du Djoué we prayed for peace during a two-week period. Some went back to the city, where Bacongo took in people from the Pool, Monganyi had residents mainly from the north, and Makélékélé and Chateau d'Eau had Pool people.

My family fled for two days on foot to Nganga Lingdo. We made it just in time to escape Lissouba's army, which cut off the Pont du Djoué. Ninjas [Kolélas militia] and others came to our village and were killing people, so we had to go farther. We were surrounded by Ninjas under the Pasteur Ntoumi, who opposed Sassou.

Banks were broken, people shot, many hurt, the women had their breasts cut off. Sassou did this. He had armored vehicles and used them. As this happened, Ninjas melted into the people. Sassou's troops attacked everywhere, calling anyone who was present a "Ninja."

My mother took ill and died in Bonya Ndanga, as there were no medical doctors left in the area. Without salt, milk, or fish, people starved. There was lots of suffering, many deaths. Random firing killed maybe up to 80,000, no one knows for sure how many.

We slept outside. People would have helped us, but they couldn't. For their own survival, some stole from people in the streets. Every day many died, including children. Helicopters came and killed all who happened to be in Ninja areas. With my mother dead, there were seven of us: my father, five brothers and a sister.

Ninja camps did their best to protect us, and took people further, to Mindouli. However, there was no food. Two of my sisters died on the way, leaving my brothers, myself, and my father. We lived like this for one year, 1997-98. As war came to our village, we moved on to other abandoned villages. Many fled. Helicopters attacked Mindouli, and all fled. Mostly civilians were killed. Sassou did this.

We fled a fourth time, this time to Bas Zaire, crossing the river over to Zaire on foot, northeast of Bacongo.

Then I got sick. My hair turned white, my body mostly bones and skeleton. Many fled to DRC, where things were a bit better. In DRC they set up camps for us, provided some medical care, then offered us rides back to Brazzaville overland. Many decided to return.

The DRC authorities also helped us cross the river by ferry, the Beach. But once we got to the Brazzaville side, men and women were separated, then most of the men were killed. My father talked his way onto the women's convoy by saying I was sick and he had to take care of me. I was in a sort of coma, weakened by dehydration. We returned to Brazzaville.

Now we were down to my three brothers, myself, and Papa. We found ourselves at the Centre Sportif de Makélékélé, taken there by bus. Lissouba had fled. We found disease and destruction everywhere. Kolélas raised the level of violence by joining Sassou. Then later, Kolélas put his Ninjas against Sassou, making things even worse. Sassou tried mediation, but Kolélas as Lissouba's former prime minister broke with Sassou, and the conflict got worse.

Angola, Morocco, Chad came in on Sassou's side, all were against Lissouba. I think they were supplied and trained by the French and by Total/Elf.

In 1994 as genocide broke out in Rwanda, Rwandans fled to Kinshasa. Former Mobuto troops came in to "clean up" the situation. Everything came from Total Oil, which took over and brought in Gabon and Chad.

Chirac said at the time, "I'd rather lose the Congolese than the Congo." The French wanted above all to prevent American oil interests from getting a foothold in the country.

[Question: Would you say Sassou is responsible for the suffering of the period?]

That I cannot say. I have told my story, the rest you will have to judge for yourself.

André's Story
U.S. Embassy security guard

I have five siblings, was employed previously at the embassy 1988-98, then laid off for ten years. I returned in 2008 and have stayed these past ten years.

When I was ten years old, I traveled by bus to Zanaga, coming from Lekoumou in the south. This was the land of Makoko [the local leader who allied with the French in the 1800s.]

I majored in French language at school, and got good training. I lost my mother and father shortly after attending school.

With the death of Marien Ngouabi in 1977, I had the idea to move to Brazzaville. After a few years there, I got to know a friend employed at the U.S. Embassy, and I was able to land a job there myself four years later in 1988.

Working from the former embassy building, I observed

the National Conference 1990-93, including the democratically verified election of 1992 when Lissouba won.

That was when the trouble started.

Sassou didn't want this outcome, and went to Oyo to brood and prepare for war. He pulled off a cynical move, convincing southerners not to cooperate with Lissouba. He supplied weapons to those on his side, and managed to return via Bacongo. His ploy got southerners killing one another, in order to block Lissouba. Bernard Kolélas played both sides, one foot with Sassou and the other with Lissouba.

Then Sassou recruited the MDCCI [Kolélas's party] to unite with [Sassou's] PCT.

Kolélas went with Sassou to oppose Lissouba—in return he wanted posts, the mayor's office, the PM position. In fact, he wanted to take the presidency from Lissouba. Sassou said to him, "You are from the south. You can become president." This convinced Kolélas to turn against Lissouba.

Barricades went up in the city in 1993. The embassy was caught in crossfire. The Americans asked us to protect property. We came under gunfire on our way to work.

In 1994, a bit of calm returned to the city. Then, shots were heard again at the embassy. Lissouba's Cocoye were on the march.

In return, Kolélas's Ninjas and Sassou's Cobras banded together against Lissouba's Cocoye. Many were killed. In this way, Sassou was able to get Kolélas's and Lissouba's militias fighting against each other. Sassou stayed in Oyo for 1995-96.

When the more intense fighting broke out June 5, 1997, our American bosses told us to "have courage and be at work." We did so. The ambassador then left us with those instructions as he and the other Americans fled to Kinshasa across the river.

We did as told. We suffered greatly. It was hard to find food, but at least we had MREs [American military "meals ready to eat"] we could draw on.

Shelling and chaos ensued, people were killed. Finally, from across the river, the Americans directed us to leave the embassy grounds. There was no safe way to do so, so we sheltered in place for three months.

Regular troops came in from ten countries: Morocco, Zaire, Angola, Rwanda, Burundi, Gabon, Central African Republic, Libya, Tanzania, Chad. Sassou had "friends" in these ten countries.

French president Chirac went to negotiate with dos Santos in Angola. Meanwhile, Elf ceased payments to president Lissouba, under directions of the government of France.

When Sassou and Chirac met in Paris in 1997, Chirac said, "I'd rather lose the Congolese than the Congo." Congo diaspora were in the meeting and heard this. When Sassou returned to Congo, French troops were sent in to help him.

Angola military intervened as well, paid by the oil company Total. Kagame of Rwanda supported Chirac, along with the ten countries Chirac brought into the conflict.

Lissouba's fatal mistakes were to raise the percentage of oil revenues going to the government of Congo (1993) and trying to arrest Sassou in 1997. Lissouba reversed his arrest order and let Sassou return to Oyo in the north, but the damage was done.

Lissouba finished his term in 1997, and elections were scheduled. One side worked up an election campaign, the other prepared for war. Lissouba was stubborn, unwilling or unable to take in information from his advisers. When the latter said "arrest Sassou," Lissouba declined, saying, "I'll defeat him fair and square in the elections." The troubles began immediately after that.

Lissouba accompanied Chirac to Gabon, not knowing that Chirac was already in league with Sassou, and Gabon's leader Omar Bongo as well. Note that Bongo was the son-in-law of Sassou, after Sassou married into the Bongo family and had a daughter.

Chirac and Bongo met in Libreville. Sassou in fact did not attend himself, but directed his representatives by phone. Here the anti-Lissouba plot was hatched, though Lissouba didn't know it yet.

June 5, major conflict in Brazzaville. The city was a no-go zone, with no one venturing out into the streets. We were caught up in the embassy and couldn't leave. I was alone there, with one other. The Americans had left, the ambassador as well.

With the war ongoing, the Americans directed us to leave the embassy, as Sassou took over the city in a military action. There was brief calm after Sassou took over.

Then the war resumed, as Sassou and the Cobra took on the Cocoye of Lissouba. Here it became purely a north-vs-south conflict. In September of 1997 Lissouba fled by car to Gabon, then from there by air to London (he was not permitted entry in France).

Cocoye and Ninja banded together against Cobra. However, the intervening countries, led by Morocco, supported Sassou's Cobra. They in turn defeated the Cocoye and Ninja, killing many.

When we were at last able to leave the embassy, I tried to get out of Brazzaville across the Pont du Djoué. A colleague and friend from the Pool got me safe haven. Since I was from the south, my friends told me the Cobras were out to kill all southerners—Bwenza, Niari, Lekoumou. They took us to be Lissouba's people, and came to kill us.

3:00 a.m. shooting broke out from near where I was staying at the Pont du Djoué. By 2:00 p.m. I figured out how to escape, and headed south. I walked fifteen kilometers, then was able to board a train on its way to the Pool. Some of us made it to Zanaga, though without any money to live on. All routes were blocked by Cobra.

The conflict was political, not ethnic!

Lissouba's military was split, among those who'd been trained previously under the Sassou regime, and others. The ones loyal to Lissouba fled to France and Kinshasa across the river.

Sassou managed to get his Cobra militia to kill southerners, and incited ethnic violence, but it was only for political gain.

The situation calmed somewhat in the city, but intensified in the provinces as Sassou's Cobra forces hunted down presumed Lissouba supporters.

I was in Zanaga. Rwandans, Moroccans, Chadians and others were there as well, killing all men thought to support Lissouba. It wasn't a battle, it was a massacre. I saw lots of dead bodies. My life was in danger.

When a driver came to town to pick up a VIP, I bribed

him with 5000 CFA francs [twenty-five U.S. dollars] to take me to Sibiti. By the time we got there, the news was that Cobra was advancing on Sibiti, so I went 166 kilometers further, on foot.

I was able to get a liter of petrol, which I managed to sell for lighting petrol lamps. My wife and children had managed to escape before then, and waited for me at Zanaga.

Lissouba was popular in that region. When he saw there were *ten* countries aligned against him, he put a railroad into operation to help people escape. Many, many went in those trains from Brazzaville to the south. Lissouba saved a lot of lives in this way.

By late 1997 I finally made it to Zanaga and was reunited with my family. But by 1998, war was everywhere.

I went to the U.S. Embassy to try to find work. I was told there was no work for me, that the White House had "downgraded" the facility. I was told this by a colleague, a northerner, our boss, who saved all the jobs for his own cronies. Twenty-four of the original ones were kept on, the others laid off for ten years.

Washington abandoned us. They said, "Don't worry, you'll be the first to be rehired." But it wasn't true. We suffered for ten years. That was how the White House left us, from then to now.

[My colleague from the north] picked his friends from the north for jobs, and let the others go. No Americans were present to fix or oversee this situation. They were across the river in Kinshasa.

In 1997 two colleagues were killed, including Ndonga Daniel, killed by a random bullet to the neck. Sopo, the embassy driver from Cameroon, put Ndonga in the car to get him to Makélékélé hospital, but he was dead on arrival. Sopo took him then to the morgue instead.

The Cobras had not yet fully taken the city, so some brave medical doctors were still at their stations. Sopo's car was filled with blood. He then took me to the Case de Gaulle [the French ambassador's residence] where we might both be safe. He left the vehicle behind and ran off. To this day, we don't know what came of him.

Also killed was Mapazzi Jean Joseph, back from annual

leave. On his first day back, he went to clear up some personal matters in Mpilou, then saw the whole city of Brazzaville was surrounded by Sassou's troops. He made it to the U.S. ambassador's [empty] residence and was killed there, his body lost without a trace.

The Americans directed us to seek shelter with family members, but this didn't happen. Militia members aimed and shot at me, but it was not my day yet, so I escaped.

Twice I escaped death: once in 1993 in a Lissouba-Ninja crossfire when I was at the ambassador's swimming pool. I saw an incoming rocket. I screamed, the rocket slammed into the swimming pool generator.

At this time, the American ambassador was very close friends with Lissouba, and went to see him, to brief him on the attack on his residence. On his way out, he handed me an envelope with 200,000 CFA francs [about $700] and wished me good luck. Later he fled to Kinshasa.

I asked then, and still do: Why did the United States never thank us, we who stayed behind? The French did so with their employees, why couldn't the Americans? But they did not.

Later I escaped death again. June 5, 1997, an incoming shell almost killed three of us, but a big tree was in the way, and the shrapnel ricocheted away from us, just in front of the embassy.

At the start, we didn't think it would be a long war. But when ten countries piled in over the course of a few months, the conflict got worse.

In 1998 things calmed down a bit, so I returned to the capital—166 kilometers on foot—only to be told that the White House had closed the embassy. As people were taken away, the embassy did nothing to stop them. The French, on the other hand, later called up their former employees who had been through the war, and in 1999 gave them medals, recognition, cash rewards. They had kept the names of their employees. Even throughout the war, their employees had safe haven if they could get to the Case de Gaulle. On our side, about seventy of us were in limbo, then later returned.

My ten years of unemployment were hard. I made it back to Zanaga but had no way to support myself and my family. In 2002 I planted a garden and did a bit of hunting. I was wasting away. In 2004 I asked if I could return to my embassy job. The answer was No. Likewise, in 2005, and the answer was No. The same in 2006, 2007. Finally, in 2008 they took me back.

The large house I had built in 1997 was destroyed. I made it through only seven months in that house. With the return of the job, I got my family back to Brazzaville, where we rented a house. In 2016 we picked up a small plot of land. Since then we've gotten our things together and built another new house. After ten years away, we're gradually getting our life back.

Whatever my age, the United States of America made me what I am. My family was restored to me. I will defend the USA to my death.

[Question: no bitterness?]

I am not bitter. What happened was not the fault of the United States. They did all they could. My bitterness is toward the politicos. It could all happen again. They caused us to lose people, property, loved ones.

[Question: whom do you hold responsible?]

In a way, all were responsible. I will say only that Lissouba was not wrong. The two sons of Kolélas, meanwhile— Parfait and Landry—drew completely apart. Both were in Sassou's government. Parfait was a civil servant for Sassou, then grew estranged and quit. Landry remains in the Sassou government, and there is no contact at all any more between the two.

Now the country declines in its economic crisis, the people suffering. We have iron, diamonds, oil—but we're all broke. Lissouba wanted to diversify the economy, to break the reliance on oil. Sadly, all the leaders want only to fill their own pockets, while the people suffer.

Democratic Republic of Congo [Kinshasa]—when DRC is sick, it comes to us across the river. And vice versa. Our Republic of Congo is small, but very tied to the DRC.

[Question: concluding thoughts?]

I would ask Western countries to keep a closer eye on Africa. Human rights—when they are abused here, Western countries should denounce the perpetrators. Here, you can be killed just because someone said something about you behind your back.

The West needs to recognize we're in a crisis. People live without water, electricity. Ignore what the government radio says!

[Question: what would you want from the West?]

I would say, don't take events in Africa lightly. The West comes in late, when there are wars and famine, but by then it's too late. Ignore the false tales of everything being ok; they're not. Keep your eye on us. Not just the Republic of Congo, but other countries also. We have good talkers here, but they twist the truth. We need genuine critics.

To conclude, I must say we are living badly here, and are a country in trouble. The government is killing the country and the economy. Westerners should prosecute criminals. The law belongs to all. Where there is lawlessness, the country does not exist.

You can give and give assistance, but when it keeps not working, just stop. It is right and well for the IMF to be hard and practical. The IMF makes recommendations to the government, then the government ignores their advice. The IMF says, "Release your prisoners, reduce the salaries of civil servants." The government doesn't want to hear this. The World Bank should oversee oil exploitation and profit sharing.

You can always tell where the rich are, by just seeing their houses. This is wrong; the country belongs to all, not just to the few.

And by the way, we appreciate President Trump's "shithole" comments, they are very good because they flush out the nature of our corrupt leaders. Stop handing money over to those in charge!

Albert's Story
U.S. Embassy employee

I was twenty-one or twenty-two years old.

The sky was heavy, dark—it was about to rain. Political tensions were in the air. The ruling party and former President Sassou were in conflict. When I woke up that day [June 5, 1997] we heard gunshots coming from the northern parts of the city—Mpila, where Sassou was staying.

People started talking, swapping rumors and information. A neighbor explained to me what could happen, that the shooting could lead to civil war.

I was scared. I went to my Grandma, and asked if I could go to Kinkala and warn my sister there not to come back to Brazzaville, where she was supposed to sit for an exam. Grandma and my father said ok, so I went to Kinkala, a bit west of Brazzaville.

There I saw the main avenues filled with civilians carrying weapons. People on the bus offered to help me. I was young and had only the equivalent of one dollar U.S.

I drank my first beer. I had to walk for miles. I had no idea how far I'd have to go. I had palm wine mixed with Primus, the local beer. There went all my money.

I walked and walked. Many others did the same, hoping to escape the conflict. In the country at least, there was still no open warfare. I was a city boy and was out of my element.

I was tired, really tired.

I made it to a village called Tiala, and climbed up and down a hill there. I was so tired. I was asking people, "Is this Tiala?" When suddenly I saw my sister.

I stayed in the village for the entire period of the conflict. I was silly, a city boy. I had no survival skills. Boys worked on plantations, but the work was too hard for me. I saw a three- or four-year-old boy with vegetables. I asked him what they were. He was amused. "Bitter roots," he said. Then he said, "Follow me, and I'll show you around tomorrow."

The next day I slept. The little boy came calling for me and took me into the forest. He guided me by the hand, showing me the roots and leaves, explaining what they were. He educated me. City boys are dumb, country boys are the clever ones.

The boy could read snake trails, ant colonies.

So in the village I was the idiot, and other boys made fun of me. I ran from the stinging ants ["fourous"] and they found this very funny. In the distance we could hear "boom, boom" all the time. Lissouba's government was firing heavy weapons; Lissouba was still fighting.

Sassou took power, and things calmed a bit. We returned to Brazzaville and found everything destroyed. Bullet holes everywhere. People were firing weapons, shooting into the air at night.

The police chief went on the radio and ordered that for a two-to-three-day period, people could shoot all they wanted into the air. But on the fourth day, they had to stop. Silence was imposed. They tried to stop the looting of the houses, especially houses of people connected to Lissouba. The call to stop looting was mainly respected.

[Question: weapons and ammunition came from where?]

From the former Lissouba army. They'd been trained by Sassou and stayed loyal to him. Also, Lissouba fired fourteen generals, which was a big mistake and turned the army against him.

Lissouba had also invited Jonas Savimbi [Angolan warlord in opposition to the Marxist ruling party] and people didn't like that. People turned against him for that.

Anyway, my family and I were ok after it was all over.

Genocide's Origin, Fear

Humans' most repellent actions come generally more from fear more than aggression, which is a symptom.

Below, a text which may make this train of thought visible. In this example, it's South Sudan instead of ROC, but the thinking is comparable. Perceived threats from South Sudan's majority Dinka population inspired the text by General Peter Gatdet Yak in 2015. Here was his manifesto, typos included:

I greet and salute all the entire Nuer community, officer and soldiers in uniform especially those who sacrifices their lives to save innocent lives of Nuer in juba.

I was so vocal to the peace which was sign between President Salva Kiir and Dr. Riek Mahcar that it will trigger another worst crisis in South Sudan which is in fact, happening now in Juba.

I was against dictatorship and tribal government which target the certain ethnic groups from sixty-five tribes of South Sudan.

We must leave our individual and personal difference and solve the Nuer problem, because what is happening is not Dr. Riek Machar's Problem, rather an entire Nuer community problem.

I urge all the Nuer youth to act immediately and take up arms to rescue their suffering families and beloved ones in UNMISS [U.N. Mission in South Sudan] camps.

I General Peter Gatdete Yak here by reaffirm my commitment to support Nuer and sided with my community and stand against any threat of Nuer existence to the point of cleansing.

I am ready to restore the lost hope and vision of the Nuer community and combat the tribal government through military means as Salva Kiir wish.

International community and IGAD [Intergovernmental Authority on Development] led peace talk should be blamed because they have failed to bring peace that address the root causes to the conflict and fail to pressure President Salva Kiir to implement the peace agreement signed last year.

(signed) Gen. Peter Gatdet Yak

Photo Gallery

Expats 1980

Arounothay (Laos) and family.

Arounothay (Laos) and Natat (Iran).

Misha and Natasha (USSR) at their first encounter with artichokes.

Mementos of 1980-82

Ministry of Information Post and Telecommunications, Department of Propaganda, Press, and Information, Division of Censorship: permission to take pictures in Congo Brazzaville free of arrest as long as the photo subjects did not include "sensitive" sites.

Dear chief of ELF Cong. staff —

Sir,

I come to your nearest high personnality in order to beg a free place in your duty as a fuel station filler up — I need that speciality because I have been studying in that domain — If that could be possible I should be more and more comforting — In waiting for your favorite answer, I want you to accept my willings —

cordialy to yours —

A student's paper, from the assignment, "Write a job application for yourself."

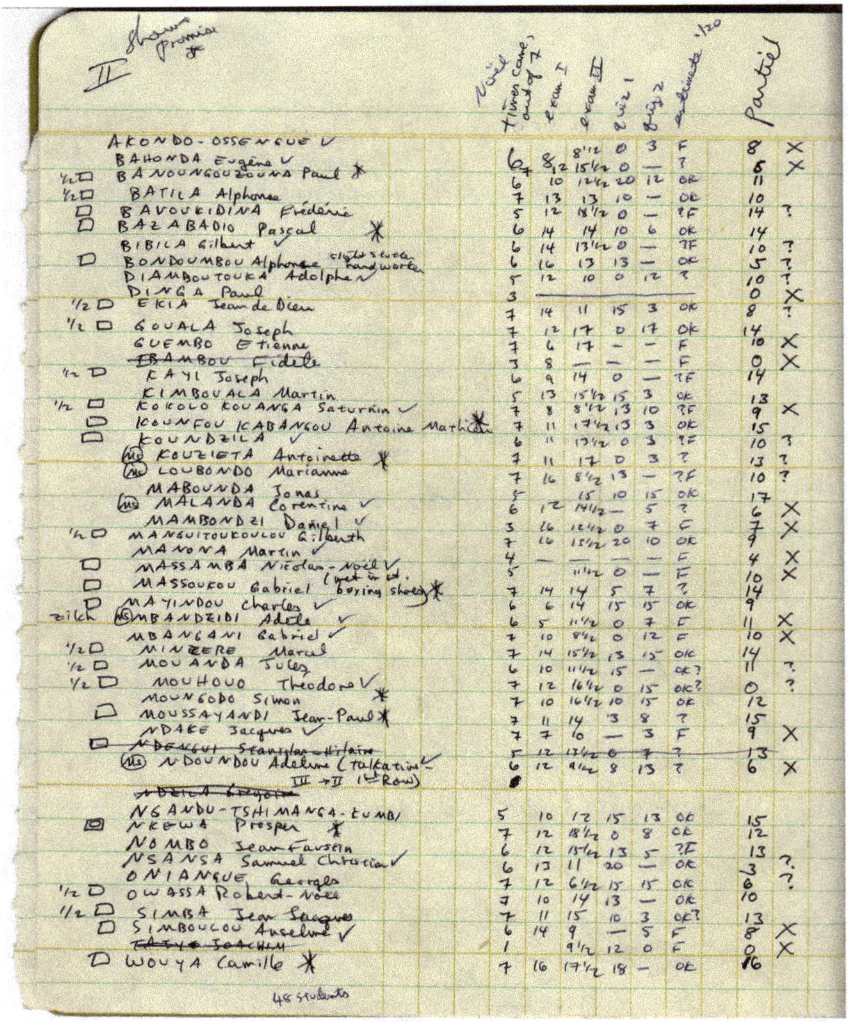

	Name	Noël		Exam I	Exam II				Partiel
	AKONDO-OSSENGUE ✓		8	8½	0	3	F		8	✗
	BAHONDA Eugène ✓	6	8½	12	15½	0	—	?	5	✗
½□	BANOUNGOUZOUNA Paul ✗	6	10	12½	20	12	OK		11	
½□	BATILA Alphonse	7	13	13	10	—	OK		10	
□	BAVOUEIDINA Frédéric	5	12	8½	0	—	?F		14	?
□	BAZABADIO Pascal ✗	6	14	14	10	6	OK		14	
	BIBILA Gilbert ✓	6	14	13½	0	—	?F		10	?
□	BONDOUMBOU Alphonse	6	16	13	13	—	OK		5	?
	DIAMBOUTOUKA Adolphe	5	12	10	0	12	?		10	?
	DINGA Paul	3	—	—	—	—			0	✗
½□	EKIA Jean de Dieu	7	14	11	15	3	OK		8	?
½□	GOUALA Joseph	7	12	17	0	17	OK		14	
	GUEMBO Etienne	7	6	17	—	—	F		10	✗
	EBAMBOU Fidèle	3	8	—	—	—	F		0	✗
½□	KAYI Joseph	6	9	14	0	—	?F		14	
	KIMBOUALA Martin	5	13	15½	15	3	OK		13	
½□	KOKOLO KOUANGA Saturnin ✓	7	8	8½	13	10	?F		9	?
□	KOUNFOU KABANGOU Antoine Mathieu ✗	7	11	17½	13	3	OK		15	
	KOUNDZILA	6	11	13½	0	3	?F		10	?
(M)	KOUZIETA Antoinette ✗	7	11	17	0	3	?		13	?
(M)	LOUBONDO Marianne	7	16	8½	13	—	?F		10	?
	MABOUNDA Jonas	5	—	15	10	15	OK		17	
(M)	MALANDA Corentine ✓	6	12	14½	—	5	?		6	✗
	MAMBONZI Daniel ✓	6	—	—	—	—	F		0	✗
½□	MANGUITOUKOULOU Gilberth	5	16	12½	0	7	C		7	✗
	MANONA Martin	7	16	15½	20	10	OK		9	?
	MASSAMBA Nicolas-Noël ✓	4	—	—	—	—	F		4	✗
□	MASSOUKOU Gabriel ✗	5	—	11½	0	—	F		10	✗
□	MAYINDOU Charles	7	14	14	5	7	?		14	
(M)	MBANDZIDI Adèle ✓	6	6	14	15	15	OK		9	
zilch		6	5	11½	0	7	F		11	✗
	MBANGANI Gabriel ✓	7	10	8½	0	12	F		10	✗
½□	MINZERE Marcel	7	14	15½	13	15	OK		14	
½□	MOUANDA Jules	6	10	11½	15	—	OK?		11	?
½□	MOUHOUO Théodore ✓ ✗	7	12	16½	0	15	OK?		0	?
	MOUNGODO Simon	7	10	16½	10	15	OK		12	
□	MOUSSAYANDI Jean-Paul ✗	7	11	14	3	8	?		15	
	NDAKE Jacques	7	6	—	3	—	F		9	✗
□	NDEKGUI Stanislas-Hilaire	5	12	12½	0	7	?		13	
(M)	NDOUNDOU Adeline	6	12	4½	8	13	?		6	✗
	NGANDU-TSHIMANGA-TUMBI	5	10	12	15	13	OK		15	
□	NKEWA Prosper ✗	7	12	18½	0	8	OK		12	
	NOMBO Jean-Faustin	6	12	15½	13	5	?F		13	?
	NSANSA Samuel Chrétien ✓	6	13	11	20	—	OK		3	?
	ONIANGUE Georges	7	12	6½	15	15	OK		8	
½□	OWASSA Robert-Noël	7	10	14	13	—	OK		10	
½□	SIMBA Jean Jacques	7	11	15	10	3	OK?		13	
□	SIMBOUKOU Anselme ✓	6	14	9	—	5	F		8	✗
	TSUYA JOACHIM	1	—	9½	12	0	F		0	✗
□	WOUYA Camille ✗	7	16	17½	18	—	OK		16	

48 students

Class Roster, 1980.

Bemba also began to tell, in hushed
tones, of how he had written Eroshima
in 1973, in his jail cell. I reminded him
of how I had never gotten that complete
story, as promised last year. Enfin, he
will visit me Thursday afternoon, and
we'll have time over the next two months
to get together. I suggested he bring his
wife & have a meal at my hotel, but
he declined on account of the "sadness
of the house" since the death of his mother-in
law last October. It was she who had
waged the battle to free him from jail in
1973, and there hadn't been a cheerful
moment since her death. ~~but right titles~~
~~remained a large exterior ~~ ~~strip morning only the wings~~
~~had removed~~ the rest.
        This morning, spent an hour on line to
get moped fuel. There was a good amount of
grumbling, sarcastic comments about "pays pétrolier".
For the past several months, apparently, it has
been this way, long lines and few service
stations having the mixture at all. Impressive
patience of those waiting in line, and none of
the jockeying for position that you would
see elsewhere. At one point we noticed
the diesel pump (15 feet away) beginning
to smoke, then leak, then smoke more
as the attendant pumped the "gasoil" into
a tractor. The same thing ran through

Journal entry, 1982.

Brazzaville 2018

The Place

The Brazza Mausoleum

The Pont du Djoué, a choke point to the city, and the scene of battles, escapes and invasions.

Congo River and pirogue.

Congo River from the Right Bank.

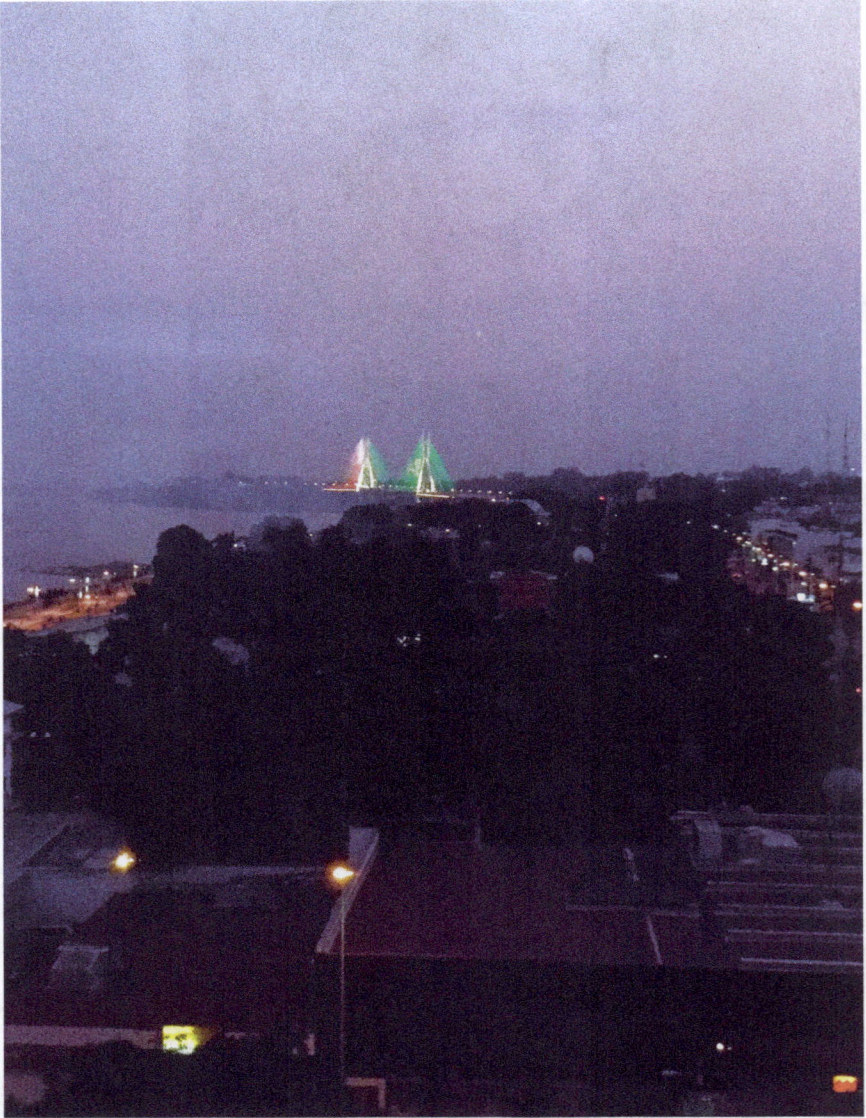

Chinese-Built Bridge to Nowhere by the Corniche, at night.

Tuesday Evening English Classes

Author and students

VOA contractor Joyce Ngoh.

Girl in Class.

Markets

Afternoon in the shop.

Woman in open market with basket.

Man sells fruit.

Woman sells fruit.

Performers

Soloist in church gospel choir competition.

The chorus bows.

Troubadour and comic Zaou parodies soldiers and the military.

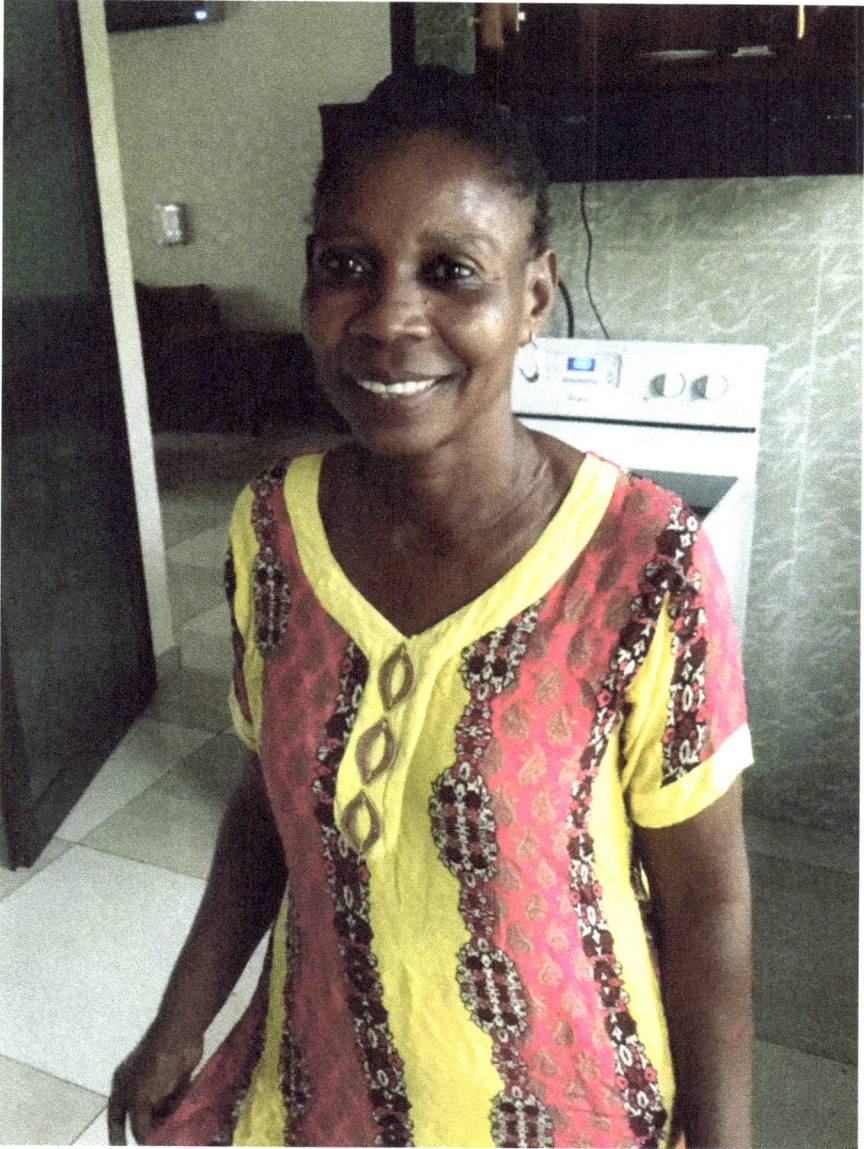

Cook and housekeeper Reine Nkondo, singing *Il pensiero* ("*Va mon amour*") from Verdi's Nabucco. August 4, 2018.

154

People

Lejuste Moukoubouka, a colleague of irrepressible talent, at La Mandarine confectionary.

Distel Kandza, the Doyen of embassy colleagues in Central Africa and beyond.

The Checkout Girl exchanged a smile for this Fort Lauderdale hat.

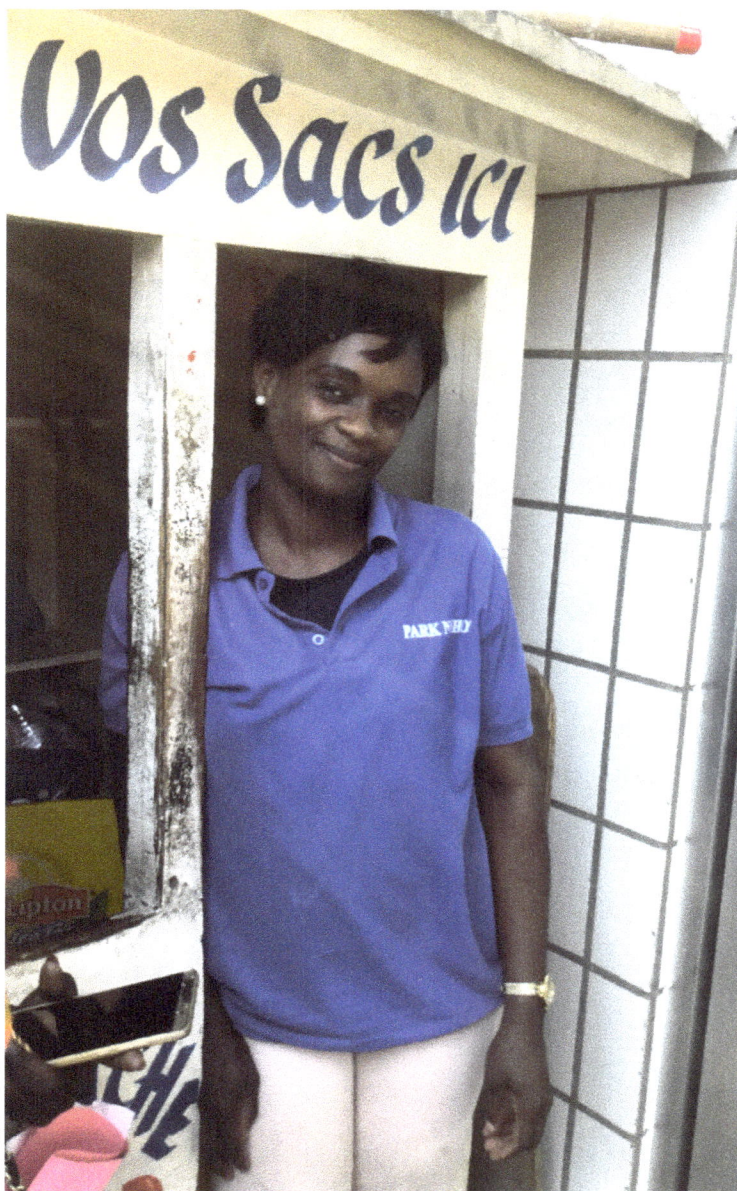

A woman named Méfiance, "Distrust".

Four

Returning in 2018

Counterpoint

August, 2018, and another moment of reflection.

After leaving Brazzaville in 1981, I'd arrived in Orly airport on summer day, and ordered a green salad at the restaurant bar. A sensuous pleasure took over: I hadn't had any leafy vegetables in a year, avoiding them so as to keep dysentery safely away. The rule was, eat nothing that grows in the ground, but only things safely far from the plant roots, like tomatoes, papayas, pineapples, mangoes. My meals had been mainly yellow: maize, spaghetti, oranges, manioc meal, eggs.

The salad at Orly was a beautiful thing and apparently the body speaks clearly about the minerals it requires. I ordered another. Then, another. The waiter started looking at me suspiciously, so I stopped at three. I would have had five, and was only partly sated after those months of lettuce-penury. I can taste them still.

I thought back to the lazy afternoons in Brazzaville by the Villa Washington pool maintained by the U.S. Embassy. They were kind to me and included me in gatherings as the only American in town not directly connected to the embassy. The embassy nurse had paid motherly attention to the Marines on their off hours, picking worms off their arms by poolside, rubbing Vaseline on their skin. This made the worms suffocate, so as they came to the surface for air, she squished them with her knowing fingers.

The only real newspaper in Brazzaville had been the Workers Party *Mweti*, "The Light." One of the editorials compared Ronald Reagan to Hitler, *"blanc bonnet, bonnet blanc."* Public Affairs Officer Bob Murphy went to the editorial offices the next day to have a conversation about this rhetoric. The author of the piece, proud of his accomplishment in getting the U.S. embassy's attention, asked Bob if he might get a U.S. government-paid trip to the United States so he could learn more.

The division of labor had been pretty clear: in a post-independence period, the Soviets chose and supported the members of the Congolese government, on the condition that they take Marxism-Leninism to heart and become advocates. Students and civil servants channeled their travel aspirations to the USSR. To them it was better than nothing. The countries they really wanted—France, the United States, and the United Kingdom—had nothing to offer them.

The French ran the economy for the benefit of anyone who had money to spend—maybe a fifth of the population. The others had to fend for themselves with subsistence farming and reselling sunglasses, cheap cutlery, and little plastic bottles of filtered water to anyone who could pay for them. Maintaining themselves couldn't have been easy in a city where they could expect no jobs, training, capital, or safety net care from an indifferent state.

The Americans were just there, in small numbers, the embassy people. No one really knew why.

Thirty-eight years later. Now in August of 2018 it was time to depart once again, and the before-and-after contrasts were dramatic. Congolese people were better fed, better informed, free of ruinous social engineering and ideological blather, but equally abandoned to their tenuous fates as before.

Same president, same genteel corruption, same exclusion of the eighty per cent who "didn't count" in a limited power structure whose main purpose was just to continue to exist. This time, though, there was something vigorous in the air. The Congolese at least had found what to think of themselves: energy, aspiration, worldliness, willingness. This still translated to the wish to get out. But when word spread that Congolese born during the French colonial period still qualified as French citizens, the planes filled up on the Brazzaville-Paris routes. People hoped for better lives as before, but now there was a sense that something better was possible. Get the government off their backs and let their entrepreneurial juices flow. Lacking that, even normal people could save and save and get a ticket to Paris, even while knowing that Africans don't do well in cold northern European cities, and aren't much welcome there.

First day on the job, 2018, I learn that President Sassou most likely *lost* his last election to his rival Youssouffa Moukoko. Two penalties for running against Sassou: first, you lose. Second, you go to jail for even trying. The country is at relative peace, though the Pool region has had low-scale skirmishes in the past eighteen months. Now refugees, homeless, internally displaced persons are mainly back in their previous homes, and food is being produced and sold. The Pasteur Ntoumi, one of the belligerents of the Pool, likely a murderer himself, and author of a "Ninja manifesto" calling for resistance to the regime, is released from prison. This leaves a good impression on Western observers, but nothing is really so simple.

Local friends tell me that "all" Congolese know this to be a ploy, and that the custom of yielding up "concessions," without even being asked, is an age-old tactic of local rulers to create and resolve crises as a way of bolstering their own power. I am reminded of the Zairian whose celebration I went to in 1979, the day he was named minister of education. Everyone in that vast front yard was jolly and downing beers. Only the minister himself was in a corner, pouting. I asked him what was wrong.

"Don't you get it?" he answered. "Mobutu appoints as ministers only the individuals he plans to destroy professionally and personally. In this country, you never say no to such an invitation, but you know you'll be arrested and sent to prison once the cheering is over."

Sure enough he was, eight months later, and held for a year until the president sensed he was repentant for ever having an independent thought. No permanent harm done, but the lesson was clear. When my friend was released the following year, he was mainly unhurt but chastised.

Likewise, it seems, for the release of the Pasteur Ntoumi in 2018 in Brazzaville. Knowing locals explained to me he had surely made a pact with his putative enemy, the president, both to defang the Pasteur and bring him into the ruling breed as a token oppositionist.

The open street markets from 1980-81 are mainly gone. Instead there are blocks of fabric shops, fruit vendors, even two supermarkets neatly arranged and filled with relatively prosperous shoppers. A world away from the marginal existences of citizens thirty-eight years before. I enter one of the fabric shops, and the owner makes a strong impression by not hassling me in any way, only responding to my queries about prices for his imported and locally woven swaths or *pagnes*. I'm not a design connoisseur, but these pieces look beautiful to me.

Compared to the scarcity of the 1970s and 80s, 2018 in Brazzaville was a relative festival. Gospel choirs competed with dazzling displays of movement on stage, coordinated choreography, and the complex counterpoint of the choir settings. Rhythms which I think could not be scanned—duple? Triple? Two-plus-threes? The fluidity of the music, constantly shifting, carried the listener with a confounding logic. Though imponderable, the meters came out as if inevitable.

I went to the Brazza mausoleum downtown, oddly the most impressive piece of architecture in the country, and devoted to a *European*. The marble palace spared no aesthetic or material dazzle. It seemed almost as incongruous as the cathedral in Yamoussoukro, Côte d'Ivoire, built by President Houphouët Boigny in the 1980s, just a bit bigger in height and length than Saint Peter's in Rome.

My second week, at the Hôtel de Ville I heard a children's orchestra with its high spirit. Some of the little players' feet did not even reach the floor. An audience including parents, teachers, representatives of embassies of Turkey, Russia, France, Germany and the United States cheered them on. The ensemble had a deficit of violas. Since I had begun my viola efforts in the same city thirty-eight years earlier, a little sentimentally I arranged to get one more viola sent from the U.S. to Brazzaville. The conductor sent queries during many months to me, asking where the thing was in transit, and I assumed it was lost or stolen on the way. But after eight months it miraculously appeared. No explanation.

July 14, the ambassador of France hosted an immense reception at his residence, formerly the headquarters of the Free French during World War II. With the German *chargé d'affaires* at my side, the thousand guests sang the Marseillaise and in quick succession, the Schiller/Beethoven theme now the anthem of the European Union. A few decades earlier, these two individuals would have been trying to kill each other.

My American colleagues told me that the seventy-five minute oratory by the French ambassador was greatly improved over the two-hour one the year before. A healthy-looking young French woman fainted not three meters from where he spoke. This didn't alter his oratory or presentation, as residence employees brought in a stretcher to carry her away, still unconscious.

That summer I paid regular visits to some of the thirty (!) local English clubs which drew young people to figure out the language mainly on their own. Unthinkable before, this now it came as a spontaneous expression of intellectual expansion beyond country and continent.

The group I saw every Thursday evening became a sort of weekly class. Fifty at a time attended, and looked to me for some native speech samples and any information I could bring to them. I asked what their ancestral myths and legends were, and how their grandparents viewed the cosmogony, the creation myth. Every culture has one. I assigned them to come back the next week and explain to me how the story went.

At the next session I listened to their admirable English as they related the Creation as told in the European Bible. I said, "Try again. I'm familiar with that one, but it's yours I want to hear about." I thought it might stimulate discussion.

Again they returned and told the same version. One of the more advanced students explained to me that any local myths or legends had probably disappeared. I urged them to find and interview the oldest member of their family quickly, before it was too late. Only a few scraps came in, from a culture now almost lost: someone called Njgami-ya-Poungou, "God Almighty," had arranged the Creation, but no one was able to tell me how.

When I asked a bit more about Njgami-ya-Poungou, the group had a frightening debate about the existence of God, and I worried about hostilities. The believers, the atheists, and agnostics were forming battalions, and I feared the outcome.

I said, "Whatever our differences, might we discuss this with open minds and friendship towards those who disagree with us?"

They all dissolved in laughter when they saw my concern. They knew, better than I did, how to differ in the best of cooperative spirit. These young people upheld their individual beliefs while maintaining closest bonds with those on the other side.

The sessions drifted in theme from God to culture to ethnicity, justice, oral history, Pascal's wager. They asked if there were witches in the United States. I quoted the Spanish proverb, *No creo en brujas, pero haberlas, haylas* – "I don't believe in witches, but I know one when I see one." They found this funny, and said it more or less matched their own approach to the matter.

The setting, the now faded Villa Washington, recalled a venue of more elegance thirty-eight years earlier. The nimble minds and agile friendships of these youngsters were indications of some moves forward, notwithstanding a dormant economy in their country which left them all just wanting to emigrate.

Snow

July. It was dry season, and mist sometimes rose at daybreak, then melted off by noon. The Congolese called this *la neige*, "snow." Like snow, the mist was light in color, came in silence and brought some cooling down from the aggressive heat of March and April.

Before, a single crude party newspaper—*Mweti*, circulation 500. Now by contrast, a bouquet of newspapers, some compromised through partial ownership of the State—some truly independent—flourish as dailies, weeklies, monthlies, and whatever else. All the real information. There is even one called *Sel-Piment* ("Salt and Pepper"), a good knockoff of the satirical *Canard Enchaîné* in Paris, artful cartoons and all. These were significant openings, though I was cautioned by Congolese that the independent ones were tolerated by the regime only to please and mislead Western observers. Congolese knew the rules, limits, and red lines—expats did not.

But even the government-owned *Les Dépêches de Brazzaville* was now reporting real news. When thirteen teenagers were killed on the night of July 22-23, 2018, in a holding cell in Cachona, M'pila, the government cover-up of police malfeasance didn't last even three days. *Les Dépêches* went into investigative mode and broke the news that police had botched the operation. This led to their conviction eight months later, March 11, 2019, where six police officers were sentenced to prison for one-to-two year terms. Unthinkable in the old Brazzaville.

Not huge numbers, but a significant handful of Congolese households had cable TV. Many of the young did not have these advantages at hand, but they well knew what CNN was, and Fox and CCTV and RT. They craved more, and the very craving is the point.

In 1980 the United States Embassy was a dilapidated fortress on the banks of the River, with thirty employees. Now there was a state-of-the-art "New Embassy Compound" with 150 busy within.

The old zoo from the 1970s exists no more, not after the war of 1997-99. The black-on-red Party billboards on roads leading the center of the city, no more. Marxism was a marriage of convenience, and served the country earlier when the Soviet Union was the only friendly nation of any importance.

The old French Cultural Center with its old dandelion puffball fountains is gone, now a bright new one in its place. Harpsichord recitals (French expats only!) from before are replaced by local arts events drawing large crowds.

The Basilique Sainte Anne, post World War II, still stands. The Pont du Djoué, though decayed, still abuts the junction of the tributary emptying into the vast Congo River. Vampire bats still lift in immense clouds from the Île du Diable at sunset, making their nightly migrations to the mainland where they can find mammals to feed on. Some things are permanent.

The tea shop under the cooling arcades from the French colonial past is now a thriving pastry shop, La Mandarine. Formerly a place of solitude for *colons* and expats, now it is filled with throngs of a growing Congolese middle class. My memory plays tricks, as I "remember" things which no longer exist.

The Brazzaville of now is half way to *désenclavement*, emerging from isolation to a wider world. This doesn't mean any of this will reach completion, but people want and expect it, and this makes all the difference.

August, 2018, my last week in the city. The woman helping in the house, Reine Nkondo, breaks into song in the kitchen, rendering a piece she has learned from her Protestant church choir. The French version goes *"Va mon amour"* but is from *"Il pensiero"* of Verdi's *Nabucco*.

The embassy has moved me from temporary lodgings to the Radisson downtown so they can spruce up the house for a new occupant, the staff sergeant arriving in two weeks.

Suddenly from the sixth floor, at the edge of a romanticized bubble, I get a view of the river from above. The sun sets, and in the distance the Chinese bridge to nowhere broadcasts in brilliant moving lights its incongruous message: *Bonne Année* and *Joyeux Noël*.

August 5, and the patio dining area serves up local greens in palm oil—*saka-saka*—and the local Primus beer. Congolese, exotic foreigners with unknown agendas, eat in the evening breeze. Behind them, the view over to Kinshasa, ominous and vast across the river, shines through the evening breezes at sunset.

The equatorial sun sinks in minutes and the meal is served on the veranda, in an abandoned bar as easily imagined in Miami. A sober sense of economic distress is in the air, and concern (not fear) of what might happen in 2021 elections.

In my room on the sixth floor in the Radisson bubble, sanitary, no smells, no sounds, only the stunning views of the city, the river, the flashing lights of the Chinese bridge.

What do citizens of poor countries want most? Surveys keep coming up with the same response: out of the options of security, jobs, health, education, housing and all of life's benefits not yet realized, justice consistently comes in first. "We can sort it out," they say. "Just remove the predators, and we'll do the rest. If you can't remove them, then at least don't have them as besties. It insults us, betrays us. We don't need your scholarships, we need only for our story to be heard and understood." All say this.

The "ethnic wars" of 1997-99 were a fig leaf for darker games by demonic opportunists. The conflicts were no more "ethnic" than the one between Caesar and Brutus. Both had militias; same ethnic, racial, religious, and geographic backgrounds, same ideology.

August 8 as I depart Brazzaville, all wait with trepidation the very overdue elections across the River. DRC President Kabila plays a waiting game for all to see, and wonder whether he will violate his many promises to the world yet again, putting himself or his wife on the ballot for the coming elections. Umbilically attached, little Congo-Brazzaville keeps a watchful eye on the colossus across the river. My local colleagues tell me that at a moment's notice, there could be *"boom boom"* as weapons are discharged in Kinshasa. Then a quarter of million DRC citizens would board every scoop and barge to escape to the Brazzaville side, putting burdens on their relatives under Sassou's governance.

Then, my own departure. On the way to the airport I learn that Kabila puts neither his name nor his wife's forward. No *boom boom* from the other side.

On to the airport, restructured by the Chinese from the former scene of our beers at dusk. The old airport remains a vivid memory, though all traces of it are gone.

The lines for embarkation are friendly, orderly. Most unexpectedly a man yields way to others in a line, instead of crowding in. This is noteworthy. I board the plane and it takes off to Paris and beyond.

Five

Renvoi

Renvoi

And a last glimpse back. When I left Brazzaville in summer of 1981, I wanted to return one day to see how people were doing. It wasn't going to be easy, but the U.S. government had a new program called academic specialists. There wasn't much else on the horizon for me, so I decided to give it a try.

Little did I know that factions formed, both for and against my return — likewise in Brazzaville and Washington. All I'd done was ask. After nine months, it turned out they did want to send me back for a couple of months, and I took them up on it for April-May, 1982.

Digging out my journal four decades later, I saw elements unlike those of the previous year. Burnished, I think. Here I offer it in parts, to fill in some blank spaces regarding daily life in the Congo. Intrigues, tastes, betrayals, reconciliations and friendships renewed strengthened my affection for the city and its people. Frustrations came again as well, and then some.

A kind of periscope brings vistas and calibrations you get with distance and the benefit of a second try. Maddening elements became more so, the charms also clearer. With extracts of the 1982 journal below, I conclude *Back to Brazzaville.*

Monday, March 29, from the plane
The last leg of my Paris-To-Brazza flight, this time landing to refuel at the Bangui airport lined with militia.

I've stepped aside as two factions battled out whether to send me back or not. It seemed to matter more to them than to me. That said, I'm glad to have another round with last year's students, assuming they'll be the ones I work with, and another chance to experience the cooler dry season.

The warm March humidity has taken hold. Those in the States who advised me not to try reliving the past will soon enough be proven right or wrong. I'll sleep and read within the familiarity of places known, ready to pick up a task not even half done before. I will seek evenings, times by myself, and the continuation of a calm I knew in Washington this past winter. With luck all will be undramatic.

In half an hour I'll find Bob at the airport and maybe a few others—Natasha? Misha? A Zopf or two? And some rest to the songs of crickets, and a meeting probably tomorrow, where I'll find out what's expected of me for these two months.

Tuesday, March 30

A heavier air and humidity I didn't remember from before. Bob M says that recent visitors who knew Brazzaville in the 1950s are shocked to see its present state. Prices have skyrocketed, just on rumors of pay raises for Congolese workers. But the raises haven't materialized, so people are doubly caught. A recent bombing of a Poto-Poto movie theater has people on edge, with talk of a Soviet plot to take down a regime too open to the West. The cinema bombing, killing twelve and injuring forty, got no mention at all in the government-controlled local press, though everyone is talking about it. Police frisk and harass people, and seem to target Soviets in particular.

My hotel room has no towel. I ask for one at the desk, but all the hotel towels are at the laundry. None to spare. The bellman shakes his head in the Congolese manner of resignation. Encrusted with sweat after my forty-eight hour journey, it seems I inspire pity.

Next morning at 7:00 the bellman goes into the city and *buys* a towel, then gets it to me. Congolese kindness.

The bathroom is reverse-engineered, sloping away from the drain instead of down towards it. This floods the area. At least the university vehicle comes on time and takes me to the department offices.

My new boss is Honoré Mabonda, I meet him for the first time. It's not too certain what my role will be in the department, but here I am, for the seven weeks remaining in the term. I meet David Mi-

landou from last year, and ask about the status of the third-year
course. He confirms my hunch that the class hasn't even met at all
so far this year, and it will be for me to pick up the loose ends.

After lunch I go to the old neighborhood and find Arounothay,
this time with his beautiful wife and daughters. His wife shows no
sign of the ordeals they've both been through under the Pathet Lao.
The Arounothays fill me in on the rumors of the city going down-
hill in the past nine months. The police harass, and the Arounothay
daughters have been sick in the uncharitable climate. So they'll be
sent home early to France.

Sad tales, like Gabriel's taking Natat and Pétra to court, claiming they had treated him roughly and hadn't paid him "in years."
(In fact, Natat had built Gabriel's house for him). In the court case,
Natat bribed the judge just enough more than Gabriel so the outcome came to nothing. Aroun, meanwhile, has had all the contents
of his shipment from France swiped at the port in Pointe Noire.
This is not like before.

Arounauthay has been burglarized twice, and had the rear window of his car stolen.

Americans gather to celebrate the fifty-ninth birthday of Dick
D of the local World Health Organization office. Yugoslavians, Af-
rican-born Indians from Zanzibar and Goa join in. Annie B, now
"plural," will go home soon while waiting for Larry's reassignment
to Riyadh.

At night I fall asleep in my hotel room to the rattle of the air
conditioner and the crackle of the short-wave radio.

Wednesday, March 31
No point trying to have cheese or croissants in my room: the
ants get them before I can.

Overcast today, with a break in the intense heat. All suggests
the dry season is still a month away.

At the university, warmly welcomed by various former students. A longer chat with the likable Mabonda. He says the snag
in my appointment was actually due to the opposition by one
member of the department, but he won't say who. Mabonda says
that as the incoming chairman, he was able to get around the issue
and sign the papers himself. I'll teach an intensive course for masters students, now in a new cycle called D.E.S. —*Diplôme d'Etudes
Supérieures*. Plus a few hours a week in the so-called language "lab,"

which doesn't have many moving parts. The idea is to lighten the load on the others, and I'm glad to do that.

I stop at the police station to get my moped insurance. The woman on duty smiles flirtatiously when I put down *"célibataire"* as my état civil. Others in the endless line wait as a document comes out for someone who isn't even in the building. The man next to me in line says, *"Pour une fois, les absents n'ont pas tort."* (For once, even the absent ones are not wrong).

Some say Yombi and his followers are suspected of the recent bombing. This may be so, though the police crackdown seems to indicate otherwise. Perhaps it's just general nervousness.

I see Misha at the department; he tells me he's gotten a letter from his sister in the USSR saying there's nothing much available at the local market there. Misha seems disgusted with life back home, and wants to stay in Congo another year if they'll let him. He's taken aback that the censors have allowed his sister's letter to reach him. Could this be sympathy at the post office, and might the system be beginning to crack?

At the Hotel Bassandza, my temporary home, I have a fish dinner—the only item on the menu. The next morning I order tea but get hot chocolate, which I guess the staff decided was what I really wanted. There is some kabuki in the way people interact here. The visitor's patience is treasured, as is the host's hospitality, it's all part of a dialectic. Something like an audience in its receptivity, energizing the performer.

Street poster:

A bas la tendance
À tirer da la société
Plus qu'on ne lui donne
(Down with the tendency to take more from society than one gives to it).

Sept heures de travail
Et non sept heures au travail.
(Seven hour work, not just seven hours *at* work).

Thursday, April 1

This morning, a big storm started around 3:00 or 4:00 a.m., and let up only at 8:00. My classes were supposed to start today, but no students showed up because of the rain overnight.

Lunch at the Bignys (Madame, the cashier at the U.S. Embassy, formerly a teacher. Monsieur, administrative assistant to the college dean). A Congolese meal of *dorade* fish, fried plantains, couscous, mandarin oranges. Talk of the educational system, the local fruits, and things in the United States, including racism and decentralized administration. Monsieur Bigny kept nodding off, weighed down from too little sleep and too much responsibility at work. It turns out they were neighbors of mine last year, though I hadn't realized it. I'm honored to be received at their home.

Then, on the moped to the old Bacongo neighborhood. Arouno-thay filled me in on more developments with the neighbors, including the ignominy of Gabriel's departure and the pathos of Harrisons' increasing isolation. Arounothay was to drive me with my belongings left at his house from last year, after my making a brief hand-shaking tour of the area. But the latter took hours, and the sun had set by the time I made it through Pétra and Natat, over to Isabelle Harrison's house. Another angle from the Gabriel-vs-Natat story came out, as Natat came back from an afternoon out: Gabriel apparently had been approached by a Congolese magistrate, who proposed they go into a partnership of cheating Europeans. Gabriel, after his years of loyalty—particularly to Natat—gave in to the temptation of some money dangled before him. The deal was that Gabriel would bring a series of Europeans into court, claiming he'd been their employee and that they had not paid him. The magistrate would judge in Gabriel's favor, then they would split the take.

Gabriel was careless enough later to admit to Arounothay that the money he had won had had to be "shared." What happened was that Natat "settled out of court," i.e., bought off the magistrate with a smaller amount of money, wanting to avoid public scandal. By the time Gabriel got his percentage of the smaller sum, he ended up with an amount he would have earned in just three months. In return he lost his job, which might have paid him in perpetuity. Then he went to rob his wife Delphine. Natat had taken out small amounts from Gabriel's salary over the years for Delphine, to make sure she would never starve. So everyone in the story lost—either money, or stature, or peace of mind.

General decline in the Congo. Prices up, thievery on the rise, open dissatisfaction with a government unable to get anything done—or even to get any fix at all on the Poto-Poto cinema bombing.

Isabelle Harrison shows me how the house's grill is now locked up for good, and explains that everyone expects to be robbed at any moment. Isabelle got as far as packing everything, getting herself a visa for Gabon and making friends promise to supply a ticket home. Then, of course, she relented when Robert begged pathetically, "If you leave me, who in Brazzaville will put up with me?"

Isabelle, apparently moved by appeals that her departure could lead to Robert's suicide, threw in the towel. Poignant, that Robert should understand so clearly the pariah he is, and how no one will have anything to do with him. I'll go soft on him these months, now that he's the underdog. Still, there are only so many times one can put up with his outrageous behavior: Arounothay reports how Robert stumbled into his house drunk last spring, pushing aside guests and accusing him of being a slave to the colonialist French. Characterizing it as Asian resolve, Arounothay recounts how he tells Harrison, "I believe you are a civilized person, and yet you come to my house to insult me. My wife and children will soon be arriving in Brazzaville, and I expect some calm. So please never come back to this house."

As for Rebecca, now absent and back for a month in Gabon, it turns out she's been told by her mother to obey Robert the European, but not Isabelle, the African. It seems she had flouted Isabelle's authority, and in any case lied to them both when it came time to bring her report card to them. Only when Robert went to complain about her being kicked out of school (accusing them of booting her only because she wasn't French) did everyone see what had been happening: she had told the school that Robert hadn't had time to sign the report card, while telling Robert the report card hadn't been issued. In the end, Isabelle was just as happy to see her sent back to Gabon. Robert had been more attached to her.

Then dinner at Arounothay with his wife and small daughters. Saturday it's a departure party and reception at Bob's for myself and three others; Sunday a bachelor brunch with Natat; then chicken at the outdoors Bacongo movie theater with Ange. Maybe I'll teach, or work, or study if I get around to it.

Pour aussi parfaite que puisse être
L'élaboration du Plan,
Ce qui est déterminant c'est
La realization

(However perfect the articulation of the Plan, what determines the outcome is the implementation).

Saturday, April 3
Today, a command appearance at the *retrait de deuil* for Ngolé, on the first anniversary of his father's death. Especially, as I'd been present at the wake a year before. The *retrait de deuil* is the one-year celebration of a person's death—sometimes as joyous as the funeral itself is morbid.

I went with no idea what this ritual really was, led to believe it was a department get-together and therefore a command performance. I arrived at 3:00 under a boiling sun, all alone at the hour mentioned on the invitation. Then Misha came, and we were the only ones there for the next hour, until 4:00. The establishment didn't want to serve drinks even when we offered to pay, plus they steered us away from seats in the shade to others, in the sun. So Misha and I went down the street for a drink. We came back and were getting ready to leave when first the Harrisons came, then some Congolese friends of the family, then Jean Pierre. This meant another hour and a half of waiting, until Ngolé's sister arrived ceremoniously, three hours late. Only then were people allowed to dance or drink.

Jean Pierre, a fine speaker, gave short talk, then Misha and I tried to escape before Ngolé's sister arrived. Now we made our conspicuous exit.

Harrison explained, meanwhile, the sad times the British Council had fallen upon. Both he and Uprichard are promised only one more year (and then, without any separation allowance when they would probably be severed in 1983-84). I asked Robert if he would try to get a local contract, but he said he'd rather starve in the UK than spend many more years here in Brazzaville. Everyone who has been here a long time claims to languish, as the Kouyoumontzakis when I saw them last night. The Kouyous will return to Marseille after next year, which will be their thirteenth. They express anxiety about that awaits them in France, as well as what awaits the human race in general.

After the *retrait de deuil* I picked up Misha and Natasha to take them over to the gathering at Bob's. The plot thickens. The ambassador and deputy were there, and there was uneasiness at having Russians at the gathering. Misha and Natasha sat forlorn while I was trying to be pleasant with the people I hadn't seen since last year.

Misha and I got Natasha home and to bed, then Misha and I went out. At the bistro we found an aggressive Brit, swilling whisky and predicting a quick end to the England-Argentina conflict which broke out last night. "Why even waste a fleet on the Argentinians," he was saying, "when we could just send it to whip the goddamn Russians."

I signaled to Misha to have only one drink and then leave, and that I'd catch up with him later. Later I found him and we discussed Man's Fate and the decay of our relative systems. Ideology overcame material weakness, he said, when the Red Russians won out over the Whites in the Russian civil war. The West lacks such a coherent reason to help it through a similar crisis, and so comes off to the outsider as just incoherence. I said self-criticism is cherished and encouraged in the West. Was that an adequate answer? Is there one?

The rain never lets up. Misha has told me that it's forbidden to engage with Westerners in the Soviet Union. Outside the country, though, they may see people as long as they account for themselves.

Next day

I visit Natat and Pétra, who are coexisting better now that Gabriel is no longer around for them to differ over. Natat admits how hard it is for those who have lived many years in Africa ever to return to France. That said, he speaks longingly for his house outside of Montpellier, which he says creates a life something like the one in Congo—in its uncluttered nature, its simplicity, and freedom from neighbors living too close.

Monday, April 6

Joachim Maoutou, the night clerk at my hotel, tells me of the Rotary scholarship he was offered two years ago for study in the U.S., and how the local ministry said he couldn't go: "If you go to the U.S., it's only so as to return as a spy." Joachim led a student strike in 1974, against Marien Ngouabi. Ngouabi had him and his allies under house arrest at the presidential palace for a month. Every other day, Ngouabi would face the group and have them state their grievances against the regime. Then he would answer and a talk would take place.

They accused him of being a *"budgetovore,"* squandering money and allowing the economy to languish, appointing incompetents to high government office under the spoils system, and never putting the military to any useful end, such as public works projects. Ngouabi solicited these comments, then accepted some and confronted others. Such fraternal discussions with students threatened by death (electrocution) only days before, seemed remarkable to Joachim, who says he ended up with affection for Ngouabi.

> *Les masses populaires*
> *Feront du Plan*
> *Un outil du progrès*
> *Social et économique*

(The masses will turn the Plan into a tool for social and economic progress).

Wednesday, April 7

Last night, Bemba's play *Eroshima* at the university, directed by Sony. The theater was jammed, standing room only. Every person was frisked on the way in, and soldiers patrolled the theater during the performance. The event could have been a choice target for whoever is out there...

The play, a series of shouts, bastonnades, grunts. Quickly tedious in its hysterical tone. It also never quite worked right technically. The lighting technician was so confused that Sony had to shout directions from the floor of the hall. At two moments—the end of each act—the audience was supposed to break out into spontaneous dance, but did not. The text seemed to echo Brecht's *Mahagonny,* and did have some interest as an African adaptation of *Mahagonny*'s tale of a community's sufferings.

In any case Bemba was delighted with Sony's directing, found it well-hewn and trim. Lasting two and a half hours with intermission, at least it was shorter than last year's dreary ordeals. The Rocado Zulu troupe had trimmed the three-act play to two. Any improvement, welcome!

There is no lack of acting talent here. Two Americans left after forty minutes, out of boredom. I was bored, too, but an occasional glimmer of brilliance kept me to the end.

I found Bemba at intermission. He told of how an official delegation of Congolese to Sofia, Bulgaria, last month had suddenly needed a fill-in, and he'd been asked to go. He'd been completely enthralled by Bulgaria. What impressed him was the frequent reference to *beauty* during the political speeches there. During one speech he was convinced it was the word most often uttered; the national version of *"Liberté, Egalité, Fraternité"* is *"Justice. Peace. Beauty."* The trip also took Sylvain on a stopover in Paris, where he visited his son, whom he hadn't seen in three years.

Bemba began to tell in hushed tones of how he'd written *Eroshima* in 1973, in his jail cell. I reminded him how I'd never gotten that complete story as promised last year. He promised to visit me Thursday afternoon and explain fully. I invited him to bring his wife and have a meal at my hotel, but he declined on account of the "sadness of the house" since the death of his mother-in-law last October. She had been the one waging the battle to get him out of jail in 1973, he said. There hadn't been a cheerful moment since her death.

This morning, spent an hour on line to get moped fuel. There was grumbling and sarcastic comments about the *"pays pétrolier."* They say it's been this way for months—long lines and only a few gas stations with the special mix for mopeds. Patience among those waiting in line, no bickering.

At one point we all noticed the diesel pump, fifteen feet away, beginning to smoke, then leak, then smoke more, as the attendant pumped the *gasoil* into a tractor. The same thing ran through everyone's mind: the attendant may be too stupid to realize the danger of an explosion killing us all. But no one wanted to give up their place in line. All were willing to risk incineration rather than leave and wait for gas later on when there might be no supply left. Finally, the French owner came out and made the attendant stop pumping. He protested, but then did so.

Lunch with a U.S. official based across the river in Kinshasa. He reports that Air Zaire is grounded again today, since yesterday's collision of two planes—not in the air, but taxiing on the runway. Also the Zairian military pilots keep forgetting to down the landing gear of their Mirage jets when landing, so now they're down from six Mirages to two. Neither fear nor shame works in the Zairian Air Force.

Two British brothers capsized in the river yesterday. The older brother had jumped into a whirlpool in the River which had sucked in the younger one. Never finding his brother, the older was sucked in himself, and nearly drowned. After about fifty seconds under water he made his way to the surface, but then was carried some twenty-five kilometers downstream, below the rapids. By this time, he found a small inner tube to cling to. Made it to shore on the Congolese side, and stayed for an hour, too exhausted to move. Congolese villagers gave him coconut milk and sent him on his way toward Brazzaville so he could report the loss of his brother to the U.S. Embassy. He couldn't speak Lari or French, and had been in Africa for only three days.

He made his way to the U.S. Embassy on foot, where the Marine guard sent him over to the consul's house. There he came upon a group watching Annie Hall on the VCR. The consul understood the Brit had lost only his boat, and invited him in to view the film. Only afterward did the whole story come out. Apparently later the brother was recovered and the story had a happy end.

> *Le Plan est la loi*
> *Et nul n'est sensé ignorer la loi*
> (The Plan is the law, and no one is entitled to ignore the law).

Thursday, April 8

Going over the McMillan anthology of American literature with my small group, I discover with my students the quirks of the Ann Bradstreets and William Byrds of early America. The students make refreshing and ingenuous remarks on the puzzling, sometimes marvelous features of Puritanism and the Great Awakening. Good source material for getting a sense of the American present as well as a colonial mentality comparable to the one my students know among the French.

Many lessons in Ralph Ellison, also, including his final refusal of politics as a way of knowing himself. Very subversive in a country such as this. Both groups understand my English perfectly; we should be able to accomplish much in these two months.

Monday April 12

> *Qui n'a pas travaillé*
> *N'a pas droit au salaire*
> (He who has not worked has no right to a salary).

Now I'm house-sitting at Dale and Thetis Hunt's house, by the Stade de la Révolution. It's a beautiful, spacious place. The Hunts' house staff Gilbert gets to work each morning perfectly at 7:00 a.m., feeding the kittens, etc. He knows better than I do what his tasks are, and seems to get pleasure and pride from doing them. I've never lived this way before. I gave him a used T-shirt to replace his rotting piece of cheesecloth. The next day he said the T-shirt had been the "rage" of his neighborhood, once he told everyone it had come from the United States.

Last Sunday, went to Easter Mass at Father Tom's church in Makélékélé. Mass in Lari, with a powerful-seeming sermon by the French priest, fluent in Lari. A demonstration of how the French have been able to hold on to this part of the world. The church was jammed, the songs spirited.

In the afternoon, unable to get anywhere near the Hunts' house, since the stadium was cordoned off for the Congo-Mali soccer match. I took refuge at the U.S. swimming pool as a storm blew over.

Went from there to Robert Harrison's fortieth birthday dinner. Malachai Quinn, as theatrical as ever and able to charm the Congolese with his interjections of Lingala. A happy affair among people who seemed to be the Harrisons' few remaining friends. It was good to see them get through a whole evening in good spirits, and without the usual scowling.

Today, sun exposure symptoms from yesterday's moped rides at midday. Light-headed, precarious stomach. I the evening, after Russian class, a militiaman stopped me for not having a headlight—my flashlight did not satisfy him.

He got friendly in an awkward way, and I saw his friendliness was going to cost me. "Three thousand [fifteen U.S. dollars] at the station, or fifteen hundred [seven U.S. dollars] with us." After I paid up, he considered us best friends, and wanted to go out for drinks and call each other on the phone all the time.

Gilbert at the house, meanwhile, has been robbed of his 11,000 CFA franc fortune [fifty U.S. dollars] and in a very pained state comes to me for help. His work is perfect, almost unbelievable, and in his case, it will be an honor to help. Theft has increased dramatically in town. Gilbert says the police are very ineffective, though at least not sadistic and violent as in other countries.

Stopped in on Natasha and Misha to drop off a book for them. They were very depressed, as their building is now to be torn down in a day or two, and they had nowhere to go. I've never seen Misha so in the dumps as he was. He kept saying, "I'm sick of everything, the heat, everything." Natasha poked fun at him but there was a despair which alarmed me. When he said "everything," I think he meant Natasha as well, and hinted he might want to come and stay in my place for a while. He tells of a recurring dream he's had for the past two weeks, where he is playing jazz at the piano, and is very happy. The dream is in color. Reality is hard on him these days.

I spoke with Mabonda in the afternoon, and he mentioned again how a member of the department (Milandou, I think) still objects to my presence here. All the more odd, since it is his skin I'm saving by teaching the course he didn't want to do himself, and is being paid for anyway.

Mabonda wants to set up a Russian language major in the department, where courses exist, but not a major. Others oppose this, seeing Russian as the language of the enemy. I didn't mention, but might, that I'm studying Russian myself at the Pushkin Institute, and don't feel that language is an "enemy."

This evening, pizza with the Zopfs, and met a Dutch UN worker, very upset over the heart attack today of her Turkish colleague. The hospital has nothing: no drugs, no clean beds, no way to ease the pain. The Turk is too critical to be moved. In essence, nothing to do.

Friday April 16

More department intrigues. At a meeting earlier this week which I managed to miss, there were more objections to my being here. Mabonda later took me into his confidence, saying he'd been glad I hadn't been there, so that some of the petty truths could come out. Two nameless colleagues had felt it was inappropriate for me to be around, though in grappling for arguments they had found no solid ones, apparently. Harrison later completed the story by naming the colleagues—Nganga and Milandou. The one thing these have in common is that I've taken instruction hours away from them by having American literature courses to teach.

The picture comes into focus: even though these courses weren't being taught before my arrival, N and M had filed for overtime, and were getting their 5000 CFA [twenty-five U.S. dollars] per course hour for having their names on the register. The other factor is that Mobonda has become a target for sniping, as a candidate from the north and selected as department chair over southerner Milandou. Now that he's at the helm, he is fair game. The unsettling thing is that Nganga and Milandou are the friendliest with me in the hallways. Of course, as far as Milandou is concerned, I'm as two-faced with him as he is with me: though I still find him friendly, evidence mounts for his being my hatchet man.

After last year's fiascos (assigning essays to students on books no longer in print, and leaving for the United States for five months without ever mentioning it to his classes, or leaving any instructions in place for work to go on in his absence), there is this year's book for his second-year class: *Uncle Tom's Children* of Richard Wright. It is a beautiful book but impossible for that group to read, with its heavy lacing of southern black dialect.

Stopped at Natasha's and Misha's yesterday, to find Natasha sitting in the courtyard like the lady on the cover of *Punch* who is packed in the movers' truck with the tables and chair. She was very sad, seemed a victim: they've been given a house by the university, only it was so filthy and ramshackle that she describes how she broke into tears when she saw it. I have a feeling they're considering going back home next year to stay.

Now looking after the two kittens left by the Hunts at their house. During a heavy downpour yesterday one disappeared, causing great consternation and grief for Gilbert and the other kitten. The missing one turned up after all three of us had given up hope.

Tonight "detained" again, while picking up my moped to see off Bob at the airport. The second time this week, and it begins to be demoralizing. This time it was a demand to see my papers, but my passport is at the Congolese Foreign Ministry waiting for a visa extension. Stopping me on a side street, the police said I'd have to pay a 12,000 franc fine [sixty U.S. dollars] I bluffed, saying they should take me to jail instead. The police held out for 3000 CFA as I resisted at 2000. When they held out for 3000, I said, *"Vous marchandez avec la justice? C'est quoi, la justice, une douzaine de mandarines?"* (Are you bargaining with justice? What is justice to you, then, a dozen mandarins?) and they laughed and accepted the lower amount. Next time I'll hold out and insist on being taken to prison.

Sunday, April 18

Something better is starting to happen—it's partly the slightly cooler weather, partly my finally jogging again, partly having finished reading *Gorky Park* and coming to an understanding with the Hunts' cats, over where they may not be and when. The viola sounds fine in this tropical foyer, though the humidity has fused the pegs to the scroll.

This evening, sought out Natasha and Misha's new place, where they'll be for a month until the real renters (a Soviet doctor and wife) come back from Pointe Noire. It was the first time I saw them since leaving Natasha depressed last week in their former courtyard, waiting for a truck to haul their things away. It's harder for me to go unnoticed in the new place. Many Soviets around, and there's no way I can get to the apartment without being scrutinized by a dozen Soviet punks and functionaries. The neighbors were at the same time helpful and intrusive, insistent on helping me find the apartment. I tried to pass as French, probably not successfully. Visiting Natasha and Misha will now be out of the question, so all will depend on their coming to visit me. They've been housed in the old Air France building, just opposite the *Maison d'Arrêt* where there was an escape this morning.

Wednesday, April 21

Yesterday I learned about the beating of the French consul general here a couple of months ago. French children were playing in the fountain in the street at the French cultural center. The police attacked them. When the consul general intervened, he was roughed up with the others. *"Vous avez giflé la France!"* he protested, and now there's been an apology from the Congolese government. However, people resented the apology: yesterday when walking my moped through a crowd of high school students, one sneered, *"laissez passer la blanc!"* I think in fact there is a mounting hostility, and now that we know the militia's rifles have live ammunition, it's only a matter of time before something nasty happens.

Had Natasha and Misha over for spaghetti last night. They said flatly that they can't have me to their new place, because of all their Soviet neighbors. I told them to come to my place, then, Tuesdays or Fridays, or whenever they can. I told them their expulsion from the nicer, earlier flat was a kind gesture of Fate, to make sure they wouldn't regret leaving the Congo when the time came. They've gone from wanting to return, to not caring, to asking not to return next year. None of us can get used to the heat.

Poet Kenneth Koch is to come May 4 for a day, and I'm supposed to arrange meetings for him.

Thursday, April 22

At lunch at the Kombans today, I learned of the INSED [Teachers Training School] disaster last week: an electric outlet sputtered. Three students, thinking it was a bomb, panicked. Two jumped out the window and fell to their death.

Tuesday, April 24

Eventless days, and a weariness of this place and an eagerness to finish up and head home. This was accented by the theft, yet again, of my moped last night. This time was inside the Harrisons' gate, within the light of the porch, not five meters from where Mike and I sat in his living room, also locked with my imported Japanese chain lock. It was out of sight only for twenty minutes. Not Congolese, but Martians must have taken it. The sad part was seeing the *line* at the police station, for all the others who had lost mopeds the same night. The country seems to inch toward Zaire in its ways, and one day may be indistinguishable from it.

Later in the evening, my lame efforts to serve up dinner—omelets—to Natasha and Misha. My organization was so bad that Natasha had to help get them in to different pot and over a different flame. While we were distracted, the cat came and got part of Misha's omelet. The bread was infested with ants. Natasha had a stomach ache and had to lie down. Then, a long and calm evening of kinship. Thoughts about the difficulty of being in touch after we are all gone from Brazzaville: will one of our dinners together be the last we will ever have?

As I write this, the arrival of a gorgeous and benign rain, much needed after two days of enervating heat.

Être révolutionnaire, c'est
Assurer le primauté de
L'intérêt général sur
L'intérêt individuel

(Being revolutionary means placing the general interest above the individual one).

Wednesday, April 26

The Hunts return tomorrow and I need new lodgings. A wretched morning tramping through the rain, looking for a hotel room—any hotel—as promised by the university, but finding none. The Olympic, which was promised to me a week ago, won't have me because they don't trust the university coupons for payment. This they admitted to me only after making me wait at the reception desk for half an hour.

So I went to the Hôtel Bassandza, where by contrast everyone warmly welcomed me. But there are simply no rooms there. I reported this all to the university's *service des relations extérieures*, where it seemed to cause a stir. They of course were furious that the Olympic would refuse their coupons. But I have no reason to doubt the man at the Olympic—vicious as he may be—when he says he flatly turned down their request over the phone a month ago, and again this week.

With the Hunts coming back to claim their house tomorrow, my only stopgap is to take up the Zopfs' offer of staying in the extra room in their house. I'll just leave the country soon if the housing question isn't somehow resolved.

Add to this my masters students not coming this afternoon because of Nganga being away and forgetting to notify me or them. They came for his class at 3:30, then left instead of waiting for mine at 5:30.

…and, this evening, the ungluing of my viola. The neck has simply broken off from the body, and the instrument came apart in my hands as I was playing it. I had loved its rich sound before this happened… I had been making some progress with third position, my goal here. It came unglued and so, I guess, did I.

Thursday, April 29

Now that things have gotten as bad as they can get, I seem to have rounded a corner where I don't care any more, and am reasonably content. After an evening with Natat, Aroun, and then Misha and Natasha, how could I be otherwise?

Spent most of the day furious at the university. They suggested putting me in the Cosmos, where the rooms stink horribly and where room 421 (mine) has hair in the supposedly clean sheets, and a filthy toilet bowl that doesn't stop overflowing.

My moped gone, I tried to get from the rectorate to the hotel and stood at the corner, looking for a taxi. A Mercedes drove up and the Congolese driver said to me in English, "Where can I take you?"

The ride took him miles out of his way, but he insisted on doing it. Seems he had overhead my ordeal at the Olympic yesterday, had been at the next table as I told Harrison my woes over a beer. He had been "*peiné*" to hear my plight and really wanted to change my feeling about leaving the country early. He had been in the Congolese foreign service, was in the first diplomatic mission to the U.S. in the early 1960s, before being a "roving ambassador" in various regions including eastern Europe. Later he'd quit, to go into the forestry business in Loubomo. He is quick to notice the weak points in the country, yet faithful to it, and duty bound to have a visitor like me leave with a good impression and consider returning.

Eddie V was stopped on his moped the other night, and fined for not paying his seven-dollar road tax. While he was discussing the matter with one policeman, another jumped on the moped and *drove off.* Just like that. Eddie waited futilely at the police station for three hours, while at least one policeman said, scratching his head, "*C'est pas correct, ça.*" The next day, the moped was delivered to his house.

Vic S of UNDP was at a bar drinking beer the other night. A brawl broke out between military and civilians. Someone attacked Vic, taking him for a Soviet and blaming him for inciting a riot. He was dragged off to jail, futilely brandishing his British passport. Here in the Peoples Republic, you only have to look like a Soviet to be hated on sight.

Tonight, a meal with Arounothay and Natat. Natat, quoting the Koran, speaks of the voyager being crazed at the beginning of a journey. This craziness he cites as the defining moment of life. He tells of how he spent three months fishing in Japan, with fifty people in a boat, playing cards in between fishing. Now that I think about it, every time I've seen Natat, he has spoken about one voyage or another.

Saturday, May 1

I'm settled now in what must be the most atmospheric hotel room in all of Brazzaville. The Beach, at the entrance to the ferry, has twelve rooms and a decent restaurant, and overlooks the river and Kinshasa across. From my tall French window, I look out onto a lush garden and the terraced restaurant a half level below. It is all 1930s colonial vintage, and lacks only Humphrey Bogart in the lobby. I am directly opposite the largest *fromager* tree in Brazzaville, or maybe even central Africa. Too distant from my room to be noisy, throngs mill around outside, changing black market money and lining up for their places on the boat with their contraband. Car horns honk and women select bananas from improvised stands. In my spacious room are two French armoires with lock and key, and a baby crib with newly changed sheets, and with two beds.

Strains of a bugle corps drift over a distant radio, bringing in live May Day ceremonies from over towards Maya-Maya. Intense preparation for May Day has gone on all week, with offices closed in the afternoon to as to give employees time to sew up their parade uniforms.

As I write this, a Congolese couple walks past my window, one yard from me, singing a popular song in Lingala.

Sunday May 2
Seeing the Hunts, my benefactors during the three weeks I took over their house, I told them their time on the beaches of the Greek islands was hard to forgive. They said they'd made up for it yesterday, by being burglarized at the Russian beach here, first by teenage amateurs who snatched their belongings and started running off with them before dropping them during the chase; outdone by a more experienced professional who broke into their friends' car and got the friends' only copies of their house keys and papers from the back seat. The race was on, to see who could get to the house first. The owners made it before the others, but had to break into their own house, since the stolen keys were the only ones.

Today, a refreshingly cool morning with café au lait by the edge of the river and some reading of Thoreau for my classes this week. From *Walden*: "There is no odor as bad as that which arises from goodness tainted."

Then a good boat trip up the Pool, with a small group of Americans, Germans, and French. Overcast enough to be pleasant.

Thursday, May 6
I'm told my frequent naps and lack of energy could be symptoms of low-level malaria.

Today, the visit by K Koch, who was good with his two audiences. Coming from Dakar and Libreville, he said Brazzaville had been his most lively stop, with the most engaging conversations.

Yesterday, after a discussion of *Walden* in my advanced class, Hélène Bengremian of Chad came up to me afterwards. Living alone like Thoreau, she said, was nothing anyone should attempt; at least, it had been torture for her for six months when she'd had to do so. This was during the civil war there, when she said Arab Chadians were seeking out Africans to kill. Hélène had fled her village after refusing to be recruited by the government. She'd needed cover to escape the government. In N'Djamena a French couple had given her the use of house, where a kindly Arab lived as gardener. She went to sleep each night expecting to be killed before morning. Hélène is convinced she went insane during those six months—understandably—and thus, even after a perceptive and sensitive reading of Thoreau's "Economy." Couldn't imagine why Thoreau would have wanted to separate himself from society even temporarily.

> *Les actes de sabotage*
> *Sont des crimes*
> *Contre le people*
> *A bas les corrupteurs*
> *Et les corruptibles*

(Acts of sabotage are crimes against the people. Down with corruptors and the corruptible).

Thursday, May 6

Today, on my thirty-eighth day here, I finally got (on loan only) a copy of my department's curriculum. It's the document without which I cannot even start my real work here, which is to write an evaluation and recommendations on the program. I have been asking twice a week since I arrived, and Mabonda always promises a copy of it for the next time we meet. Finally, he relented today and did so.

Two golden-souled waiters at my hotel restaurant, which is to close forever tomorrow after forty years in operation. The one tells of the Zairian thievery techniques, whereby they come at night with a magic potion to put the victim into a deep sleep, then remove all his belongings, sleep with his wife, and sometimes as parting shot, shave his head. The theft, minus the shaved head and the rest, had been my waiter's own experience. The other man, the partner, is a clown, a poet, and mime artist. In a hall empty of other customers, he brings out his own dinner to display a heaping handful of prepared manioc wrapped in a palm leaf: *Béton armé.* He says he recommends me to the Holy Spirit in his prayers, since I'm the only client here who ever leaves a tip.

Saturday, May 8

The dilemma is whether to pay the long-outstanding electricity bill from a year ago, so as to make amends for the current occupant who refuses to pay his part. Legally I can't leave the country without proof that "my" bills are paid, even though my lien is from a year before.

V, the current resident of my house of a year ago, is like Rineheart of *Invisible Man*: Wherever I go, I meet people he's rubbed against—in his, case, the wrong way. He accuses Arounothay of being "so tight-fisted he squeaks," when clearly it's the reverse. He complains of Arounothay's servants taking showers at the house, when it is Arounothay—not V—who pays the water bills. I dread having anything to do with him. Yet we have to work out a deal to get the water bill paid so I will be allowed to leave the country. He's less motivated since he'll stay longer this year than I will.

Yesterday the new assistant at the embassy came into my hotel bar with Leon Dash of the *Washington Post* here on assignment. Lots of fawning going on around Dash, from American staff. Since his falling out with Ambassador Oakley in Kinshasa, paranoia prevails here, to the point where the American community was convened at the embassy for a "confidential" briefing. Not privy to the briefing, I was filled in by at least three who were there. Comically, RC is telling Dash about the local dishes you can get in Brazzaville, and the names of a few places where you can get them. When he sees Dash pull out his little notebook to jot them down, RC gets concerned: "Now you realize, this is all *off…the…record.*"

Dash, looks at RC, realizes he has an idiot on his hands, looks at me, and shrugs.

Yesterday Natat and Arounothay rescued me from the hotel and took me to a Congolese place up the north road. During the drive back, Natat told of the plight of a French friend who produces local yoghurt. The price of milk has tripled in recent years, but the government won't let yoghurt go above sixty-five CFA (thirty cents

US) per jar. The reason: the Frenchman hasn't been able to gather the extortion money—20,000,000 CFA ($10,000 US)—to get government permission to raise the price. Nor can he go out of business, or lay off workers, since it's illegal for a European to lay off Congolese workers. The Frenchman keeps on keeping on, waiting for the time when he'll get the 20,000,000 CFA to pay off the government.

> *Le plan Quinquennal*
> *Est la volonté*
> *De désenclaver l'arrière pays*
> (The Five-Year Plan will bring the back country out of isolation).

Today took my first test in Russian, and was pleased. I understood nearly everything, though I fizzled on the dative of personal pronouns.

Tuesday, May 11
Not a drop of water at the hotel, due to work on the main line outside. It looks like a move to Deputy Chief of Mission AR's house—my sixth Brazzaville residence in two months.

Thursday, May 13
So now after a day of no water at the Beach hotel, where every day I go to see the women load their contraband like actresses being made up backstage, now I am at the DCM's palatial house. I will leave soon enough. A day of waiting: waiting for the electric company to admit they lost my dossier, waiting for the insurance company to admit they'd done the same, and waiting for police interrogation of me to come to an end, as a faded picture of Yassir Arafat ("Founding Father"?) glared over my shoulder: and waiting an hour and a half for my own embassy in its confusion to get a key to me for the DCM house.

Now all is calm, and I've made it through the neck of the bottle. Through adversity one grows to love a place—enough adversity only, that is, to be drawn into the smell and muck and to become part of the scent. How could I ever hate Brazzaville, with chunks of myself all over the city, at every street crossing and half the villas? I'd have to hate myself.

I meet Bernard Nganga as he finishes his half of the class we share, and as I arrive for my half. We exchange greetings. Asked about the next week's schedule, and he magnanimously enough offers the class to me for next Wednesday and Friday, seeing as how he will be out of town in Pointe-Noire for a week. I gratefully accept, knowing that next week will be my last here, and that I need the extra hours with the class.

As I begin the class, I announce this slight change, telling them we'll have a double session next Wednesday, and the usually two-hour session on Friday. They look around at one another, some-what embarrassed. "Well you see," says one, "We won't be here. We're all going to Pointe Noire with Monsieur Nganga. We'll be gone for a week."

Sunday, May 16

I'll be partly sorry to leave next week. The DCM's house is a luxuriant sanctuary, where I'm awakened in the morning by soft ecclesiastical chant at the convent, or whatever is next door. The days are soft now, the weather cool. Brooding and still, grey skies like the ones I like North America for in November begin most mornings.

Tuesday, May 19

Now, everything goes right. After losing my electricity receipts altogether, the SNE at last has given me a *quittus* for a scant 13,000 CFA [seventy U.S. dollars] when in fact I probably owed ten times more. Everyone seems to agree, it's a fair trade for the toil I've gone though. I "donated" my moped to the Congo, now in exchange I get off with the 13,000 for permission to leave the country. I walk through the streets like a Congolese, with my red umbrella as a parasol, becoming a city fixture. And the beautiful canticles awaken me in the morning.

Last night, the last evening with Natasha and Misha. We sat by the poolside of this place, and ate fish left in the refrigerator by Charles the Beninese cook. Natasha and Misha came laden with presents, a Russian grammar book and a picture book of the Mos-cow Metro. They come up in a taxi, a *"cerceuil avec da la musique."* (musical coffin).

We talk about how we will try to stay in touch in the future. They say that even after three years here, they have no Soviet friends they can trust well enough to transmit messages or packag-es from me to them next year.

Lunch at noon today with Roger and Arlette Chemain, who are savvy and fond of their lives. Stupid, that I didn't get to know them better last year.

And tonight, the touching occasion of Vice Rector Makosso-Makosso taking me out for a meal at the Mistral, in gratitude for my having taken him out the year before in Washington, and also for my months here in Brazzaville this year. Makosso's wife also came, and M Mahondza, the author of my woes of early May, and my boss Mabonda of the Foreign Language Department. A perfectly gracious and intimate event. It if it was intended to extract some forgiveness for the gruesome week in early May, it succeeded.

We joked, among other things about Zaire, the shameful cousin. The one about the peasant hit up by the police and producing every form of ID card conceivable. The policeman, exasperated and running low on funds at home, said, "And your profession?" The man answered, "Peasant." "Well then," said the policeman. "Well then, let's see your *carte d'agriculteur!*"

So he got his extortion money at last.

At the end of the meal, Makosso turned to me with the slight formality of the lovely African custom, and recited a speech to underscore the meal's being in my honor, and thanking me for my services. At one point he referred to *"certain moments difficiles,"* or *"certaines défaillances"*. All I could do was wince and nod no, and return his speech with one of mine, speaking of the Congo as my second home. I didn't have to lie to say so.

Friday, May 21

Finally got my exit visa. I should have timed the final process: I think it took less than sixty seconds, after fifty hours of waiting, and weeks trying fix things to avoid mishap.

I am resolved to what is happening, not like last year. There is a craft to farewells, which blends the willingness to move on with the creation of time and single-mindedness for the people one is fond of. It's the only important thing I have to do during the next forty-eight hours.

Saturday, May 22

A student waits at my door for three hours in the afternoon sun, wants to hand me his take-home exam a week late. When I arrive, he shows me his copy of the book: he has loaned it to a "colleague," and had it returned with the last fifty pages missing (the subject of the essay).

As for love of children: Marcelle Yengo's sister, giving birth, calls for help to the midwife just as the baby's head is appearing. The midwife says she is tired, and that it's time for lunch. She departs.

Myths to demystify, legends to verify. If they ever get to where they want to here, it will be only after facing the things in their culture which are lies.

Yesterday, farewell at the Pushkin Institute, after my last lesson there. The director and a couple of colleagues, and Misha, clustered around and we exchanged lame but well-intentioned jokes about my trip back to the capital of imperialism, and the gangsters of Rostov being tougher than the "bandits of Tchicago." The staff loaded me with books—Gorky readers in English.

The staff at the DCM house say they have prayed to God that I be sent on a permanent mission to Congo. Gilbert of the Hunts' house was waiting at the house when I go back this afternoon, after trekking from the Hunts to see me before I left. We sat and talked on the back patio, then shared a taxi to Bacongo.

And this evening, the last of my stay. I had said to Misha to come over today, and of course he and Natasha got first preference since I may never see them again. He has said several times that they're not allowed to fraternize with westerners once they're home in Rostov-na-Donu. It won't be easy for them there, as it has been more or less in Brazzaville. I waited for them most of the afternoon and into the evening. They were at their weekly accounting meeting at their embassy, where Misha was presented with something like a "most valuable player" award for his work at the embassy teaching French to the Soviets.

While I was waiting, GD came over to invite me to dinner. I had to explain to him why I wanted to stay and wait where I was. He, too, wanted to meet Natasha and Misha. Soon GD and his guests were over at my house with the lavish French meal Chantal had cooked at home.

As we were all finally sitting down to eat, the bell rang, and there were Natasha and Misha. When they saw other people there, they made gestures to leave, maybe fearing an ambush. I didn't force them in at first, not wanting to put them in jeopardy. Then when I saw their objections were more social than political, I insisted they come in.

Things loosened up a bit, and Misha charmed the French and B and V. People trailed off, and the three of us were finally left together.

We walked a good bit of their way home, stopping before any of their embassy mates might see them. We were all sentimental, but Misha most of all. Misha pissed some of his beer behind a tree in front of the Hôpital Général. I followed suit, after getting him to point out the spot he had used. Natasha suggested we put up a plaque at the site, designating the tree as *Pamyatnik Druzhbih*—the Monument of Friendship.

Knowing we might never see one another again left with a numb ache and even fear of what it will be like when anesthesia wears off after surgery. We walked silently without a word, for a long way. It was now two o'clock and the streets were deserted.

Finally, a taxi came to take them off, but not before we all embraced, and like imbeciles under the abandoned moon made our groggy, separate ways.

Bibliography

Anderson, Mary B., Dayna Brown, and Isabella Jean. *Time to listen: Hearing people on the receiving end of international aid.* Cambridge, MA: CDA Collaborative Learning Projects, 2012.

Ayittey, George. *Africa Unchained: The Blueprint for Africa's Future.* New York: Palgrave Macmillan, 2005.

Boyd, William. *Brazzaville Beach.* New York: Harper Perennial, 1990.

Calderisi, Robert. *The Trouble with Africa: Why Foreign Aid Isn't Working.* New York: Palgrave Macmillan, 2006.

Cohen, Herman J. *The Mind of the African Strongman: Conversations with Dictators, Statesmen, and Father Figures.* Washington, DC: New Academia, 2015. (ADST-Diplomats and Diplomacy Book).

Conrad, Joseph. *Heart of Darkness.* First published UK: Blackwood's Magazine, 1899.

Dongala, Emmanel. *Un fusil dans la main, un poème dans la poche.* Paris: Albin Michel, 1973.

"Duel to the Death," *The Economist.* April 8, 1999, www.economist.com/node/320717.

Dumont, René. *L'Afrique noire est mal partie.* Paris: Seuil, 1962.

Easterly, William. *The White Man's Burden.* New York: Penguin, 2006.

Easterly, William. *Tyranny of Experts: Economists, Dictators and the Forgotten Rights of the Poor.* New York: Basic Books, 2013.

Hochschild, Adam. *King Leopold's Ghost: A Story of Greed, Terror, and Heroism in Colonial Africa.* New York: Macmillan, 1998.

Hooks, Aubrey. Interview by Charles Stewart Kennedy September 5, 2009. Association for Diplomatic Studies and Training. www.adst.org

Jahn, Janheinz. *Muntu: The New African Culture.* New York: Grove, 1961.

Kapuscinski, Ryszard. *Travels with Herodotus*. New York: Vintage, 2008.

Loutard, Tati. *Anthologie de la littérature congolaise d'expression française*. Yaoundé: Editions Clé, 1977.

Mills, Greg, Jeffrey Herbst, Olusegun Obasanjo, and Dickie Davis. *Making Africa Work*. London: Hurst and Co., 2017.

Moss, Todd, Caroline Lambert, Stephanie Majewrowicz, *Oil to Cash: Fighting the Resource Curse through Cash Transfers*. Washington: Center for Global Development, 2015.

Moyo, Dambisa. *Dead Aid: Why Aid is not Working and How There is a Better Way for Africa*. New York: Farrar, Straus and Giroux, 2009.

Naipaul, V.S. *A Bend in the River*. New York: Penguin/Random House, 1979.

National Museum of African Art. *Selected Works*. Washington: National Museum of African Art, 1999.

Phillips, James. "Oil, Blood and Steel: The Failed Attempt to Create a Democratic Congo." Interview by Charles Stewart Kennedy. Association for Diplomatic Studies and Training, May 5, 1998. https://adst.org/

Petringa, Maria A. *Brazzà, A life for Africa*. Bloomington: Author House, 2006.

Racine, Daniel. *Homage Posthume a Léon-Gontran Damas*. Paris: Présence Africaine, 1979.

"Republic of Congo Second Civil War," Global Security, December 31, 2016. www.globalsecurity.org/military/world/war/congo-b.htm

Revel, Jean-François. *Ni Marx Ni Jesus*. Paris: Robert Laffont, 1970.

Sachs, Jeffrey D. *The End of Poverty: Economic Possibilities for Our Time*. New York: Penguin, 2005.

Sylvain, Bemba. *Rêves portatifs*. Dakar: Les Nouvelles Editions Africaines, 1979.

Sylvain, Bemba. *Tarentelle noire et diable blanc*. Paris: Editions Pierre Jean Oswald, 1976.

Sylvain, Bemba, and Léopold Mamonsono-Pindy. *Bio-Bibliographie des écrivains Congolais*. Brazzaville: Editions Littéraires Congolaise, 1979.

Tansi, Sony Labou. *L'Anté-Peuple*. Paris: Seuil, 1983 (Grand Prix de l'Afrique Noire).

Tansi, Sony Labou. *La Vie et demie*. Paris: Seuil, 1979.

Tansi, Sony Labou. *Les Sept solitudes de Lorsa Lopez*. Paris: Seuil, 1985.

Tansi, Sony Labou. *L'État honteux*. Paris: Seuil, 1981.

Tansi, Sony Labou. *Les Yeux du Volcan*. Paris: Seuil, 1988.

Tansi, Sony Labou. *Qui a mangé Madame d'Avoine Bergotha?* Paris: Editions Promotion Théâtre, 1989. [Inscription, "Pour mon frère hébreux Dan Whitman, en pensant toujours à la tribu perdue, Paris 2/10/90.]

Twain, Mark. *Kind Leopold's Soliloquy*. Boston: P.R. Warren, 1905.

Vansina, Jan. *Oral Tradition: A Study in Historical Methodology*. New York: Penguin, 1961.

Wauthier, Claude. *L'Afrique des Africains: Inventaire de la Négritude*. Paris: Seuil, 1964.

Acknowledgements

With grateful recognition to the Association for Diplomatic Studies and Training for permission to excise interview transcripts on line (www.ADST.org) for Ambassadors James D. Phillips, 1998, and Aubrey Hooks, 2009.

Acknowledgment also to the *Foreign Service Journal* for their kind permission to reprint the introduction, "Back to Brazzaville," in its October, 2019 issue.

For their help and encouragement, I am indebted to Todd Haskell, Katja Hering, Kari Jaksa, Ilya Levin, Bernth Lindfors, Asunción Sanz, Stephen Schwartz, Vladimir Pimonov. Gratitude to my five interviewees for coming forward.

Special and exceptional thanks to Susan Golden and Fatima Montero Navarro.

www.ingramcontent.com/pod-product-compliance
Lightning Source LLC
Chambersburg PA
CBHW061731270326
41928CB00011B/2189